The Four Ingredient Cookbook® Holidays and Celebrations
ISBN 978-0-9789638-0-4

Copyright 2007
Publishers: Linda Coffee and Emily Cale
Coffee and Cale
P.O. Box 2121
Kerrville, TX 78029
1-800-757-0838
Fax: 830-895-5568
Wholesale Orders: 830-895-5528
www.fouringredientcookbook.com
Send e-mail to the authors at:
Linda Coffee: linda@fouringredientcookbook.com
Emily Cale: emily@fouringredientcookbook.com
For sales questions e-mail Bob Cale: areglen@ktc.com

Yoli Graphic Design and Full House Productions

To all our busy friends and families who still want to get together and celebrate.

A special thanks to Emily's mother-in-law, Wilma Cale, who has been indispensable in helping us put together this book.

About The Cookbooks

In 1990 Linda Coffee and Emily Cale wrote their first cookbook, **The Four Ingredient Cookbook®.** Genuinely amazed and pleased with the instant success and the urging of customers asking for more, the ladies kept creating and testing new recipes. They have now authored and published a series of **Four Ingredient Cookbooks**. Each cookbook contains recipes (only with four ingredients) from appetizers, salads, vegetables, main dishes and desserts.

The Four Ingredient Cookbook® - Volume One… the original cookbook which contains over 200 four ingredient recipes. A great tool for busy families, singles, students, campers…just about everyone!

More of the Four Ingredient Cookbook® - Volume Two… more four ingredient recipes from appetizers, salads, vegetables, main dishes and desserts.

Low Fat & Light Four Ingredient Cookbook® - Volume Three… recipes especially selected to help reduce fat and still taste great! Nutritional analysis is given for each of the recipes.

The Four Ingredient Cookbooks®: Three Cookbooks in One… the first three cookbooks combined into one larger convenient cookbook. Contains over 700 four ingredient recipes.

The Diabetic Four Ingredient Cookbook®… this large print edition contains 352 four ingredient recipes with the nutritional and diabetic exchanges for each recipe. There are over 180 recipes that are low in carbohydrates and conveniently marked by a "Low Carb" icon.

This new cookbook, **The Four Ingredient Cookbook® Holidays and Celebrations** is the sixth in the series. Linda and Emily hope that folks will find it easy to use and helpful as they celebrate with family and friends.

Dear Friends and Family,

We are still on a quest to make life simpler! Whether it is family, old friends or new acquaintances coming to dinner, we find that entertaining can add stress to our lives. Often, the challenge is just trying to figure out what to serve our company! We have found that lack of time for planning often makes entertaining even more difficult. Our goal was to provide the planning, to help simplify the marketing and preparation, so that you won't have to spend your time. We have prepared full menus, easy recipes (each with only four ingredients) and shopping lists for each party to serve eight adults.

We entertain at specific times throughout the year, often in connection with a holiday or special event. So, we selected some of the different holidays and celebrations for our menu themes. We hope you will find these menus, simple four ingredient recipes, and shopping lists to be a helpful tool that will allow you to plan, prepare, serve, and most importantly, ENJOY hosting your own dinner parties.

Linda Coffee and Emily Cale

Table of Contents

Section One: **Holiday Menus, Recipes, and Shopping Lists**

Section Two: **Recipes by Categories**

Entertaining Tips, Ideas, and Décor

Food Safety and Food Tips

Entertaining Tips, Ideas, and Décor

Thanks to our friends and family who shared some of their decorating and entertaining ideas

Linda and Emily

Icebreaker: A fun icebreaker party I throw is to have the guys make their favorite appetizers and to bring the recipes. Have the ladies do the judging. You can have different categories and then give a prize to each. For example, the most attractive, the over all best, creative, meat, vegetarian, and sweet/dessert type. *Carol Martin*

Wonderful Guest!: When I am invited to someone's house for dinner, I write a short thank you note and take along a pretty refrigerator magnate. Right before I leave and when the hostess is not looking, I place the thank you note along with the magnet on their refrigerator. This makes a nice surprise for the hostess when she is cleaning up. *Deda Garlitz*

Centerpiece Cupcakes: For a party, I ordered chocolate and vanilla cupcakes with all white cream frosting. I arranged the cupcakes on large fancy trays with paper doilies and decorated them with edible flowers I bought at the grocery store. I then added the leftover flowers to the trays at random. They also served as beautiful centerpieces and were the topic of conversation. They were easy to serve and could be easily accessed by the guests. *Gloria Garoni*

Summer Table Decoration: For table decorations, I like to save empty, small perfume bottles. I pick flowers from my garden in the summer and place one flower in each bottle and set one at each plate. *Mar Porter*

Summer Beach Party Table Decoration: For a summer beach centerpiece, place a large colorful umbrella into a coffee can packed with sand. This will allow the umbrella to stand in place. Place more sand in the middle of your table with coffee can in the center. Bury coffee can with more sand and slightly slant umbrella. Scatter seashells around the top of the sand. *Debbie Jacoby*

Summer Garden Party Table Decoration: For a garden party or outdoor summer party, use cantaloupes and honey dew melons as luminaries. Slice and scoop out the melons, cut out a design of your choice, and place a votive candle down into the center. *Barbara Buckles*

Valentine's Table Decoration: On Valentine's Day, place a white table runner on the table with one main large object, like a candelabra, in the center. Decorate and intertwine with Valentine garland down the center of the table. Then add additional items down the center such as candy boxes standing on their sides, family pictures in small picture frames, small vases of red and white flowers, heart candles and smaller red, white and pink candles. *Alice Whatley*

Bring A Friend For Valentine's Party: I cut placemats from white textured wallpaper and then overlay them with Valentine tissue paper. I used pink and white flowers and lots of ribbon and long strings of pearls like you find at Christmas time. Tied pretty ribbons on napkins and my place cards were pink hearts. I also asked each guest to bring a friend that I might not know. This was neat meeting new people and lots of fun. *Ann Huie*

Easter Table Decorations: I place small Easter baskets at each place for place card holders. I also add small treats to the baskets for my guests to take home. *Carol Martin*

Fall Centerpiece Decorations: In the fall, I pick up fallen, colorful leaves and spread them around the middle of the table with tea lights intermingled. *Mar Porter*

Fall Table Decorations: I tie two or three pieces of wheat together with raffia and place onto different fall colored napkins at the table. Decorate the table using pumpkins, gourds, and/or fall flowers, clay pots with nuts and seeds spilling onto the table. *Barbara Gaither*

Tea Light Pumpkins and Gourds: For a party in the fall, decorate the table with all sorts of pumpkins and gourds (different sizes) and carve a small hole in each of them to place a tea light candle in each one. *Jan Robinson*

Mini Pumpkin Centerpiece: Display vegetable and mini pumpkins on a tray. Fill in gaps with fall leaves, moss, straw or wheat. *Barbara Hix*

Bobbing Apples Decoration: Fill a large bowl that you want to use as a centerpiece with water. Place several apples into the water to see how they balance and float. Mark the tops of the apples with a dot. Place a tea light over the dot and trace around the tea light. Using a knife, carefully cut into the apple vertically as deep as the tea light is tall. Place the tea light into the apple and float the apples in the bowl of water. *B.J. Grayson*

Fall Place Cards: Use large thick fall leaves, like Magnolia leaves. Using a felt tip pen, write the names of each guest on the leaf. *Debbie Jacoby*

Acorn Place Card Holders: Hot glue clusters of acorns and place a place card in between one or two of the acorns at each place setting. *Dodi Pressler*

Halloween Party Tip: Make a spiced apple cider and put dry ice into it. It smokes and looks scary. *Kim Coffee*

Thanksgiving Tablecloth Decoration: Purchase a large, white or ecru tablecloth and some colored markers for fabric. Trace an outline of a large leaf in autumn colors- one for each of your guest. Ask your guest to sign and date and write something about some of the things for which they may be thankful. Follow the instructions on the markers for preserving the colors and each year add to the leaves and signatures. The tablecloth becomes a memory "scrapbook" of our Thanksgivings together. *Lisa Carpenter*

Winter Table Decoration: In the winter, I cut small branches off my evergreen trees and shrubs, especially the ones with berries, and spread them out with a couple of ribbons intertwined and a few candles. *Mar Porter*

Christmas Guest's Gifts: When I have a Christmas party, I like to have something for my guests to take home with them. Make or buy inexpensive Christmas tree ornaments, hang them on a small, special tree in the entry by the door and tell your guest to take one as they leave. Or, if you have a lot of people coming over, you can just get small, glass balls, personalize them with a glitter paint pen and put them in a large, pretty bowl or basket. It's a nice way to thank your guests for coming to celebrate the holiday season with you. *Ashli Guild*

Christmas Wine Tags: I create my own Christmas wine tags by using last year's Christmas cards. Punch a hole in the top, thread with a colorful ribbon and tie to the wine glasses. You can add details by layering shapes, using paper punches and scalloped scrap booking scissors to add style. *Barbara Gaither*

Christmas Stocking Napkin Holders: At Christmas time, I use small Christmas stockings at each place for napkin holders. You can write your guests name on them. Example, use glue and glitter to write the names on. *Carol Martin*

Silver and White Christmas Table Decorations: At Christmas time, I like to use silver charges, white and silver china, three large and two small silver trees sitting in snowflake wreaths, snowflake candles, and small silver tree candles for place cards. Use lots of silver and white ribbon. I also hang silver Christmas balls and ribbon from the chandelier. *Ann Huie*

Tea Light Decorations: For a fun table, hollow out coconuts or pineapples and fill with water, float tea lights in the shells. If you don't want to use fruit, choose a pretty dish on a pedestal and fill with water and flowers and float tea lights. To add a tropical flair, top the table with a sarong or pareo from the beach and dress with shell necklaces. Also at Christmas, try floating the tea lights in a hurricane filled with cranberries and water. *Linda Imel*

Chair Décor: Tie netting around the backs of your dining room chairs and then tie a big bow in the back for an added festive flair. This is also a good way to camouflage folding chairs when you have a large crowd for dinner. *Alice Whatley*

Candle Holder Idea: If you don't have votive candleholders, use glass tumblers filled with cranberries or other items for an extra splash of color. *Dee Dee Sheridan*

Frosted Fruit: To make a pretty centerpiece use frosted fruit. Simply dip whole fruit in a beaten egg white, then into sugar. Let dry. *Kim Coffee*

Herb Centerpiece: Instead of flowers as your centerpiece, use fresh herbs as your flower arrangement. Or, mix fresh herbs with flowers. *Barbara Hix*

Package Centerpiece: Cover your table with a tablecloth using a color scheme of the season. Then tie a grogram ribbon in a large bow around the middle of the table to make the table look like a present. You can add additional touches like scattered leaves in the Fall, stars for the Fourth of July, or small ornaments or balls at Christmas time. *Karen Snowden*

Double Candle Holder Idea: Take a tea light and place inside a short glass votive holder. Find a larger glass holder, like a wine glass, and put some craft pony beads (or gravel, sand, marbles, etc.) on the bottom. Place your tea light in the smaller holder inside the larger holder and fill up the space between with your beads. I used colored beads in bright colors that coordinate with my Christmas tree ornaments. Do several with outer containers of different heights for a festive effect. *Christie Kitchens*

Chalkboard Menus: For dinner parties I like to have a mini menu at each place setting for each guest. Sometimes I write the menu on a small chalkboard and place it near the centerpiece. *Ann Huie*

Photo Wine Tags: Cut out pictures of your friends and punch a hole into the tops. Thread them with a ribbon and tie to their wine glass. *Jenny Stanley*

Organizational Tip: To save time and not feel rushed, get out all your serving platters and bowls and put a note on each one with the name of the dish that you will be using it for. *Lisa Carpenter*

Guest Bathroom Tip: When having a party, don't forget your guest bathroom – use scented candles and make sure there is an extra roll of toilet tissue. Decorative paper hand towels are also a nice touch. *Barbara Hix*

Ladies Birthday Table: For a ladies birthday party, I use different colored bows in my flower arrangement representing different birthday months of the ladies present. Also, I use the different colored ribbon for the napkin rings and have the ladies sit according to their birthday months. For example, you can say, January is red etc. *Carol Martin*

Hawaiian Party Idea: For a Hawaiian party, bake an angel food cake and put dry ice in a small container into the center of the cake before bringing the cake to the table. It will smoke, like a volcano. *Marlene Carbine*

Mexican Theme Table Setting: When having a Mexican dinner party I use my Mexican pottery dishes and blue glasses with yellow napkins stuffed in them. Mexican piñatas on wooden dowels with Mexican flowers make colorful centerpieces. *Ann Huie*

Western Horseshoe Decorations: If you want to set a table outside and it's a little windy, I put the paper plate down, then the napkin, and lay a (clean) horseshoe down (with the shoe facing up for good luck). I have some old horseshoes I spray painted gold, but the rusty look is good too. You can spray a clean rusty shoe with clear varnish if you like. I let people take the shoes home as a party favor. *Christie Kitchens*

Western Theme Table Decorations: Use bandanas as napkins for a western theme on your table. For the centerpiece, use an old cowboy boot and place a vase inside the boot. Fill the vase with fresh flowers. Place the boot on a bandana or tie a bandana around the boot. *Debbie Jacoby*

Western Outdoor Barbeque Tablecloth Tip: When you are having a outdoor barbeque and it is a little windy, hold your tablecloth down by taking old spurs and fastening them around a table leg. Then pull the fabric through the spur letting the spur show. *Christie Kitchens*

Italian Party Candleholders: For an Italian dinner party, use empty Chianti bottles as candleholders. Use candles that drip because the look of the wax on the bottles is good. Tie a grape bunch from the craft store on the bottle. Additional centerpieces to go along with the Chianti bottles can be a pretty bowl of grapes and a tray of cheeses. *Cheryl Knowles*

First Course Entertaining Tip: A tip I use in serving the first course of my sit down dinner, is to serve it to my guests while they are still standing up. Often, when we call our guests to be seated for dinner, they seem to hesitate for quite awhile. They are usually deep in conversation and do not respond to the hostess. Serving soup in a long stemmed wine glass allows them to continue talking while helping the hostess to begin serving the meal on time. Of course, clear broth or creamy soups work best. Serving the soup this way seems to add a little more class to your party. *Lorraine Wilson*

A Practical Wine Tag Tip: When I entertain, instead of messing with wine tags, I save "odd" wine glasses and let my guests pick the wine glass that they want. It is also a fun collection to collect and to have! *Sandy Merritt*

Mix and Match Tip: For a beautiful table, mix and match china patterns using same color schemes. *Wilma Cale*

Plate and Punch Cup Collection: I collect the glass punch cups and plate sets that were popular in years past and are now available at yard sales, flea markets and thrift stores for reasonable prices. In a short time, I have collected over 100 sets and use them for bridal luncheons and teas, baby showers and anniversary parties and been happy to loan them to friends and family for their special events. I keep them packed in plastic tubs, so that they are ready to be easily transported. They do fine in the dishwasher and they are inexpensive enough that if one gets broken- no one needs to feel badly about it! *Loma Bammel*

Silver Flatware Gift Idea: My parents and grandparents began giving pieces of silver flatware at Christmas and for birthdays when we were very young. We each have many place settings; and since we all have the same beautiful pattern, we can share when we need larger amounts for parties. A tradition I hope to continue for my children! *Jayne Zirkel*

Frosted Glass Rims: Frosting on the rims of drinking glasses adds to the party atmosphere. Dip the rim of the glass into a small bowl of water, and then dip into sugar. For added color, tint the sugar. *Jenny Stanley*

Wine Glass Markers: You can buy packages of thin, wire hoop pierced earrings at your local craft store. They clip on perfectly to the wine glass stem. Decorate them with small, inexpensive charms and beads (also sold in packages at the craft store). You can also get small, alphabet beads and put your guests name on the wire so each guest has their own personalized wine glass. Cute, inexpensive and fun. *Ashli Guild*

Basket Utensil Bundles: Even an informal barbeque can be dressed up. Instead of just having a tray with your plastic cutlery in it (or even shoved in plastic cups, as I hate to say I have done), you can wrap a fork, spoon and knife in a paper napkin and secure it with a cute ribbon or raffia. Put all the utensil bundles in a pretty basket. *Ashli Guild*

Buffet Party Tip: If you are having a buffet style party, put a cute place card by each dish, labeling what it is. I can't tell you how many close calls I've had with people allergic to shellfish almost eating the crab appetizer! *Ashli Guild*

Party and Recipe Swap Idea: If you are having a potluck, have your guests bring some copies of the recipe of their dish to place by their food. Now its not only a potluck, but a recipe swap as well. *Ashli Guild*

Landscape Your Centerpiece: After preparing a delicious meal, it can be made all the more enjoyable by presentation. Use interesting bowls and platters, and try to set a nice "landscape" for special meals. Vary the heights of the dishes, and use a few decorations fitting for the meal or season. *Jan P. Thomas*

Fantastic Easy Party Dessert: When it warms up in South Texas, I have a favorite, easy dessert for a party. Scoop vanilla ice cream in a pretty sherbet or champagne glass and serve to each guest. Bring out all your 'after dinner' liqueurs on a silver tray, and let each guest pour their favorite over the ice cream - Kahlua, Amaretto and Chambord are always good - but just about any flavor will work. If you want to add fresh fruit, strawberries or ripe peaches add some color and wonderful flavor. If someone's watching their weight or sugar intake, they can just pour a little bit of liqueur over the fruit and skip the ice cream. I'll usually pass homemade truffles or other chocolates, since there's always someone who needs their chocolate 'fix'! *Tina Woods*

Flavored Water Tip: For every tea/luncheon I serve carbonated flavored water with a coordinating fruit in each glass. For example, cran-raspberry water with fresh raspberries. Most grocery stores carry a brand of flavored water. Served in a beautiful pitcher, it appears part of the decoration. What is nice is the water is sweet, low-or-no calorie, refreshing, and does not stain if spilled. Most people would never guess it was grocery store flavored water. *Renee Abel*

Food Safety:

Food safety places a vital role in entertaining. There are four simple steps that are critical in food safety:
- Clean: wash hands and surfaces often;
- Separate: don't cross-contaminate;
- Cook: cook to proper temperatures;
- Chill: refrigerate promptly.

We have found a food thermometer is an essential cooking tool. It takes the guesswork out of knowing when the food has reached the correct temperature. Remember temperatures should be taken at the thickest portion of the food. Listed below is a chart of meat thermometer readings:

Raw Food	Internal Temperature
Hamburger	160 degrees F
Beef, veal, lamb, pork	160 degrees F
Chicken, turkey	165 degrees F
Roasts and steaks	
medium rare	145 degrees F
medium	160 degrees F
well-done	170 degrees F
Pork chops, roasts, ribs	
medium	160 degrees F
well-done	170 degrees F
Ham, fresh	160 degrees F
Sausage, fresh	160 degrees F
Chicken, whole & pieces	180 degrees F
Duck	180 degrees F
Turkey (unstuffed)	180 degrees F
whole	180 degrees F
breast	170 degrees F
dark meat	180 degrees F

For more information on food safety, the USDA website has a wealth of information. www.usda.com

Food Tips

Cool Whip Measurements:
8-ounce container of Cool Whip contains 3 cups of Cool Whip;
12-ounce container contains 4 1/2 cups of Cool Whip;
16-ounce container contains 6 1/2 cups of Cool Whip.

Remember white wine taste best when it is slightly chilled. So put your white wines in the refrigerator the morning of your party.

Sweeten your whipped cream with confectioners sugar instead of granulated sugar. It will make it fluffier.

To keep the oil in your oil based salad dressing from settling at the bottom of the bowl and keeping it on your greens, take the dressing and heat it in the microwave for ten seconds before using.

To keep your celery crisp, wrap it in aluminum foil when storing in the refrigerator.

When working with dough, don't flour your hands; coat them with olive oil to prevent sticking.

When using skewers for grilling and using foods with different cooking times (such as shrimp and beef), don't combine them on the same skewer. Instead, make skewers of just shrimp or just beef, start cooking the beef first, then the shrimp, and then combine them on a serving platter.

When making kebabs, use two skewers instead of one. Kebabs of meat, shrimp or vegetables cook more evenly and are easier to turn if you pierce the food with two skewers. This way, when you turn the kebabs with tongs, the food doesn't spin around the axis of a single skewer.

Warm your dishes in the oven before putting hot food on them. This will help keep the food warmer longer. For an outdoor cookout in the summer, place your platters or bowls of cold food on a larger bowl or bucket filled with ice to help keep them cool longer.

Use a piece of steel wool to sharpen your kitchen shears.

If your family is coming and you are running behind making dinner, sauté some onions and your kitchen will smell wonderful and homey.

Don't break eggs directly into batter. Break into separate container. To remove any eggshell, use a larger piece of eggshell to attract the piece in order to remove.

Lemons stored in a sealed jar of water will produce twice the juice.

Cheese won't harden if you butter the exposed edges before storing.

When separating eggs, break them into a funnel. The whites will go through leaving the yolk intact in the funnel.

For a perfect boiled egg, cover eggs with cold water and a pinch of salt. Bring the water to a full boil. Remove the pan from the heat and cover. Let the eggs sit for 15 minutes. Drain the hot water and run cold water over the eggs.

When picking a melon, smell it for freshness and ripeness. Check to see that the fruit is heavy in weight and that the spot on the end where it has been plucked from the vine is soft.

Ground spices should really be replaced every 6 months or so.

Don't throw out leftover wine. Freeze into ice cubes for future use in casseroles and sauces.

A dampened paper towel or terry cloth brushed downward on a cob of corn will remove corn silk.

If your cake recipe calls for nuts, dust nuts with flour before adding to the batter to keep them from settling to the bottom of the pan.

Meat slices more easily when partially frozen.

To keep cauliflower white while cooking, add a little milk to the water.

Lettuce keeps better if you store in the refrigerator without washing first so that the leaves are dry. Wash the day you are going to use and wrap in a damp paper towel. This will crisp the lettuce.

Microwave garlic cloves for 15 seconds and the skins slip right off.

When baking potatoes, set them end up in a muffin tin. They can be removed from the oven all at once and checked for doneness. Also, it makes it easy to drop them into a serving basket without burning your fingers.

Keep adhesive labels and a permanent marker in your silverware drawer to easily remind you to mark your food with a date before you put it in your freezer. It will work by taking the guess out of "How long has that been in there?" and "What is that?"

Keep a ruler in your kitchen drawer. When you need to measure a baking dish or check the size of diced vegetables, the ruler will be handy.

Before measuring honey in a glass-measuring cup, coat the inside of the cup with a light film of canola oil. The sticky honey will slide out.

When you need to wash shredding cheese off a pan or plate, remember to use cold water. Hot water will spread, stretch and gum up the cheese.

Substitute long sliced vegetables, like carrots or celery, for a rack under a roast if you do not have a metal rack to place your roast on.

To keep delicate sauces warm without burning, after it is cooked, place the sauce into a thermos until ready to use.

To tint coconut, place in a jar with a lid and add a few drops of food coloring, and shake until evenly tinted.

Foods to keep handy in your pantry or refrigerator for those unexpected last minute guests are: cheese and crackers, chips and dips, cookies, nuts, wines and soft drinks.

Holiday Menus,

Recipes, and

Shopping Lists

New Year's Eve

New Year's Eve is a time we celebrate. It is a time to reflect on our past and look forward to our future. We cherish our families and friends. We wish all of you a Happy New Year and hope these recipes will help make planning your celebration a little bit easier. Happy New Year!

Linda and Emily

Bubbles and Beads

Black Bean, Roasted Red Pepper Pate

Stuffed Mushrooms

Artichoke Pesto Gratin

Olive Martini Appetizers

Bleu Cheese Walnut Salad

Rosemary Roasted Pork Tenderloin

Spinach Casserole

Buttered Herbed Pasta

New Year's Eve Rolls

Sparkling Fireworks Dessert

Bubbles and Beads

We suggest you start this party with an easy Champagne drink. Have your champagne glasses ready for your guests when they arrive by placing a few dried cranberries in each Champagne glass. When your guests arrive, pour the Champagne over the cranberries and serve immediately. The cranberries will float around the glass.

Black Bean, Roasted Red Pepper Pate

1. **1 Can (15 oz.) Black Beans (rinsed and drained)**
2. **1/2 Cup Roasted Red Peppers**
3. **1 Package (8 oz.) Cream Cheese (softened)**
4. **1 Tablespoon Regina Champagne Wine Vinegar**

In food processor, combine above ingredients and blend until smooth in texture. Place in a serving bowl, cover and refrigerate until ready to serve. Serve with Melba toast rounds or assorted crackers.

Stuffed Mushrooms

1. 1 Pound Fresh Whole Mushrooms (half dollar size)
2. 1 Cup Bread (cubed into very small pieces)
3. 3 Tablespoons Butter (melted)
4. 2 Slices Sandwich Ham (chopped into small pieces)

Preheat oven to 350 degrees. Clean and remove stems from mushrooms. Chop stems and place into a bowl. Add cut up bread, melted butter and chopped ham. Mix well and stuff into mushroom caps. Place mushrooms onto a lightly sprayed casserole dish and bake at 350 degrees for 15 minutes.

Artichoke Pesto Gratin

1. 2 Cans (10 oz. each) Artichoke Hearts (drained)
2. 1/4 Cup Sundried Tomato Pesto
3. 1 Cup Shredded Romano Cheese (3/4 cup in mix and 1/4 cup for top)
4. 1/2 Cup Mayonnaise

Preheat oven to 350 degrees. In food processor or blender, chop artichokes. Add pesto, 3/4 cup Romano cheese and mayonnaise. Blend for 5 seconds. Place into a lightly sprayed 9x13-inch glass-baking dish. Sprinkle remaining 1/4 cup cheese over top and bake at 350 degrees for 20-25 minutes or until bubbly. Serve hot with roasted garlic panetini bread.

Olive Martini Appetizers

1. **1 Jar (10 oz.) Jalapeno Stuffed Olives**
2. **1 Jar (10 oz.) Garlic Stuffed Olives**
3. **1 Jar (10 oz.) Calamari Olives**
4. **1 Jar (10 oz.) Anchovy Stuffed Olives**

Drain and place each of the different types of olives into four individual martini glasses. Serve with festive holiday toothpicks. **Serving Idea**: Place the four olive martini appetizers on a decorative silver tray.

Bleu Cheese Walnut Salad

1. **2 Bags (5 oz. each) Spring Mix Salad Greens**
2. **2/3 Cup Walnut Halves**
3. **1/4 Cup Bleu Cheese Crumbles**
4. **1/4 Cup Raspberry Walnut Vinaigrette Salad Dressing**

Combine salad greens, walnut halves, and bleu cheese crumbles in salad bowl. Cover and refrigerate. Before serving the salad, toss with the Raspberry Walnut Vinaigrette Salad Dressing.

Rosemary Roasted Pork Tenderloin

1. **4 to 5 Pounds Boneless Pork Loin Roast**
2. **1/2 Cup Coarse Grained Mustard (we used Grey Poupon Country Dijon)**
3. **3 Tablespoons Balsamic Vinegar**
4. **2 Tablespoons Fresh Rosemary (chopped)**

Preheat oven to 375 degrees. Spray roasting pan with cooking spray and place roast into pan. Combine mustard, balsamic vinegar and rosemary. Spread over roast and bake at 375 degrees for 1 1/2 hours. Internal temperature needs to reach 160 degrees. Let stand for 10 minutes before serving. Place onto serving platter and garnish with fresh rosemary sprigs.

Spinach Casserole

1. **1 Package (8 oz.) Cream Cheese (softened)**
2. **1 Package (16 oz.) Frozen Chopped Spinach (thawed and well drained)**
3. **1 Can (8 oz.) Sliced Water Chestnuts (drained and chopped)**
4. **1 Package (1.4 oz.) Knorr Vegetable Recipe Mix**

Preheat oven to 350 degrees. Mix cream cheese, vegetable mix, and water chestnuts with drained spinach. Place into a lightly sprayed baking dish and bake at 350 degrees for 25 minutes.

Buttered Herbed Pasta

1. 1 Package (16 oz.) Wide Egg Noodles
2. 3 Tablespoons Butter
3. 1 Tablespoon Fresh Italian Parsley (chopped)
4. 2 Tablespoons Fresh Chives (chopped)

On stovetop, cook pasta according to package directions, al dente (pasta should be tender, but still firm, not mushy). Drain, and while pasta is still hot, toss with butter, fresh Italian parsley and fresh chives. Serve warm.

New Year's Eve Rolls

1. 2 Cans (11 oz.) Refrigerated Pillsbury French Loaf
2. 1/2 Cup Butter (melted)
3. 1 Tablespoon Italian Seasoning
4. 1 1/2 Teaspoons Garlic Powder

Preheat oven to 350 degrees. Remove bread dough from cans and slice each bread dough roll into 6 equal rounds. Place each slice on shallow baking dish or jelly roll pan. Combine melted butter, Italian seasoning and garlic powder. Brush each slice with butter mixture. Bake at 350 degrees for 20-25 minutes or until golden in color.

Sparkling Fireworks Dessert

1. **1 Bottle (1 oz.) Orange Extract**
2. **8 Sugar Cubes**
3. **1/2 Gallon Vanilla Ice Cream**
4. **Chocolate Syrup**

Place ice cream balls into eight individual serving dishes. Top with chocolate syrup. Pour orange extract into a small condiment dish. Toss each sugar cube individually in the orange extract making sure cube is well saturated. Place one sugar cube on top of each ice cream ball. After all guests are served, using a long stem lighter, light each sugar cube. Orange soaked sugar cube will flame for a very effective New Year's finale. **Helpful Hint**: You may want to practice lighting an orange extract sugar cube, so you will know what to expect. **Helpful Hint**: The day before, freeze scoops of ice cream balls and place on wax paper in an airtight container. Place in the freezer. Margarita glasses make a festive serving dish.

Serving Idea: Place a large basket with roasted garlic panetini bread, melba toast or assorted crackers on a table with the bowls of the Black Bean Pate and Artichoke Pesto Gratin.

New Year's Eve Shopping List

Produce

- __ 1 Pound Whole Fresh Mushrooms (half-dollar size)
- __ 2 Bags (5 oz. each) Spring Mix Salad Greens
- __ 2 Tablespoons Fresh Rosemary
- __ 1 Tablespoon Fresh Italian Parsley
- __ 2 Tablespoons Fresh Chives

Bread, Crackers, Chips

- __ 1 Cup Bread
- __ Roasted Garlic Panetini Bread
- __ Melba Toast
- __ Assorted Crackers

Meat

- __ 2 Slices Sandwich Ham
- __ 4-5 Pounds Boneless Pork Loin Roast

Pantry Items

- __ Dried Cranberries
- __ 1 Can (15 oz.) Black Beans
- __ 1/2 Cup Roasted Red Peppers
- __ 1 Tablespoon Regina Champagne Wine Vinegar
- __ 2 Cans (10 oz. each) Artichoke Hearts
- __ 1/4 Cup Sundried Tomato Pesto
- __ 1/2 Cup Mayonnaise
- __ 1 Jar (10 oz.) Jalapeno Stuffed Olives
- __ 1 Jar (10 oz.) Garlic Stuffed Olives
- __ 1 Jar (10 oz.) Calamari Olives
- __ 1 Jar (10 oz.) Anchovy Stuffed Olives
- __ 2/3 Cup Walnut Halves
- __ 1/4 Cup Raspberry Walnut Vinaigrette Salad Dressing

- __ 1/2 Cup Coarse Grained Mustard
- __ 3 Tablespoons Balsamic Vinegar
- __ 1 Can (8 oz.) Sliced Water Chestnuts
- __ 1 Package (1.4 oz.) Knorrs Vegetable Recipe Mix
- __ 1 Package (16 oz.) Wide Egg Noodles
- __ Sugar Cubes (at least 8 cubes)
- __ Chocolate Syrup

Spices

- __ 1 Tablespoon Italian Seasoning
- __ 1 1/2 Teaspoons Garlic Powder
- __ 1 Bottle (1 oz.) Orange Extract

Frozen and Refrigerated Products

- __ 2 Packages (8 oz. each) Cream Cheese
- __ 2 Sticks Butter
- __ 1 Cup Shredded Romano Cheese
- __ 1/4 Cup Bleu Cheese Crumbles
- __ 1 Package (16 oz.) Frozen Chopped Spinach
- __ 2 Cans (11 oz. each) Pillsbury French Loaf
- __ 1/2 Gallon Frozen Vanilla Ice Cream

Miscellaneous

- __ Champagne
- __ Cooking Spray

New Year's Day

People celebrate many different traditions on New Year's Day. We celebrate by eating black-eyed peas for good luck and green cabbage for wealth. After celebrating during the Christmas holidays, we tried to keep the recipes for this day easy and simple. Sit back and You and your family enjoy!

Linda and Emily

Smoked Salmon Log

Black-eyed Pea Salad

Cabbage and Bacon Salad

Tropical Fruit Salad

Dijon Glazed Corned Beef Sandwiches

Cookie Stacks – Gingerbread Cookies; Nutty Lemon Cookies, Chocolate Peanut Butter Cookies

Chocolate Fondue

Individual Chocolate Peppermint Coffee

Smoked Salmon Log

1. 1 Package (8 oz.) Cream Cheese (softened)
2. 1 Package (4 oz.) Smoked Salmon (flaked)
3. 2 Tablespoons Green Onions (finely chopped)
4. 2 Tablespoons Celery (finely chopped)

Combine above ingredients and shape into a log. Refrigerate until ready to serve. Serve with assorted crackers.

Black-eyed Pea Salad

1. 2 Cans (15.8 oz. each) Black-eyed Peas (drained and rinsed)
2. 1 Medium Red Bell Pepper (cored and chopped)
3. 1/2 Medium White Onion (chopped)
4. 1/4 Cup Vinaigrette Salad Dressing

In serving bowl, mix above ingredients and chill at least one hour or overnight in refrigerator. Season to taste. Toss before serving. Serve cold.

Cabbage and Bacon Salad

1. **1 Small Head Cabbage (chopped into small pieces)**
2. **1 1/2 Cups Sharp Cheddar Cheese (cut into small cubes)**
3. **10 Slices Bacon (cooked and crumbled)**
4. **3/4 Cup Roasted Garlic Rice Vinegar**

In serving bowl, mix above ingredients and chill at least one hour or overnight in refrigerator. Season to taste. Toss before serving. Serve cold.

Tropical Fruit Salad

1. **2 Jars (24 oz. each) Del Monte Tropical Fruit (drained)**
2. **1 Cup Green Grapes**
3. **1/2 Cup Walnut Pieces**
4. **2 Tablespoons Creamy Poppy Seed Salad Dressing**

In serving bowl, mix above ingredients and chill at least one hour. Gently toss before serving. Serve cold.

Dijon Glazed Corned Beef Sandwiches

1. **2 Containers (13.8 oz. each) Refrigerated Pizza Crust**
2. **1 1/2 Pounds Deli Sliced Corned Beef (3/4 lb. on each dough)**
3. **2 Packages (8 oz. each) Sliced Baby Swiss Cheese (1 package on each dough)**
4. **1/2 Cup Dijon Mustard (1/4 cup on each dough)**

Preheat oven to 400 degrees. Use two lightly sprayed 9x13-inch baking sheets. Place one crust on each baking sheet. Pat and spread dough until it is approximately the same size as the pan. Top each pizza crust with a layer of corned beef down the center of the dough. Top corned beef with a layer of cheese. Spread the mustard over the top of the cheese. Repeat layers ending with the mustard. Fold dough over the top of the meat and cheese and pinch dough together to seal. If necessary, moisten the dough with water to help seal. Repeat this process on the second pizza dough. Bake the sandwiches at 400 degrees for 20-25 minutes or until dough is golden brown. Remove and place sandwich rolls on wire rack to prevent bottom from being mushy. When slightly cooled and ready to serve, use a pizza cutter to slice into sandwiches.

Cookie Stacks

We are giving you three very easy cookie recipes to use for this day. We suggest you serve these cookies on a platter, and then with the remaining cookies, divide them among your guests, stack them on top of each other, wrap them in plastic wrap and tie them with a bow. Cookie stacks to go. **Suggestion**: Cookies can be made ahead and stored in airtight containers.

Gingerbread Cookies

1. **1 Box (10.25 oz.) Moist Deluxe Spice Cake Mix**
2. **1 Teaspoon Ginger**
3. **2 Egg Yolks (room temperature)**
4. **3/4 Cups Butter**

Preheat oven to 375 degrees. In mixing bowl, cream the butter and add the egg yolks and continue to mix. Add the ginger and cake mix into butter and yolks, and mix until well combined. Dough is very stiff. Place dough on a lightly floured surface. Pat dough into a flat circle. Cover with a sheet of wax paper; and with a rolling pin, roll dough out into 1/8-inch thickness. With a round cookie cutter, cut cookies and place 2-inches apart on a lightly sprayed cookie sheet. Bake at 375 degrees for 10 minutes or until slightly browned. Remove to wire rack to cool.

Nutty Lemon Cookies

1. 1 Container (16.5 oz) Refrigerator Sugar Cookie Dough
2. 1 Cup Chopped Pecans
3. 1 Tablespoon Grated Lemon Peel
4. 3/4 Cup Powdered Sugar

Preheat oven to 375 degrees. Place cookie dough into a mixing bowl. Add pecans and lemon peel and stir until well blended. On a sprayed cookie sheet, drop cookie dough by tablespoon (walnut size) and bake at 375 degrees for 10-12 minutes or until very lightly browned. Cool 2 minutes on a cookie sheet and then remove to wire rack. Place powdered sugar in a bowl and dip warm cookies in the powdered sugar. Place back on wire rack and cool completely.

Chocolate Chunk Peanut Butter Cookies

1. 1 Jar (18 oz.) Peanut Butter
2. 1 1/4 Cups Sugar
3. 2 Eggs (room temperature)
4. 1 Bag (10 oz.) Dark Chocolate Chunks (Nestle)

Preheat oven to 350 degrees. Combine peanut butter, sugar and eggs in a mixing bowl. Beat with mixer until sugar becomes smooth, about 3 minutes. Chop chocolate chunks into smaller chunks and combine with the peanut butter mixture. Form into about 1-inch balls and place onto an ungreased cookie sheet. Press down on the center of each ball and bake at 350 degrees for 10-12 minutes or until lightly browned. Remove from oven and cool on a wire rack.

Chocolate Fondue

1. 1 Package (12 oz.) Semisweet Chocolate Morsels
2. 3/4 Cup Whipping Cream
3. 1 Bag (8 oz.) Peanut Brittle
4. 1 Bag (10 oz.) Pretzel Rods

In a medium microwave safe bowl, combine chocolate morsels and whipping cream. Microwave on high for 1 minute, stirring once. Remove from microwave and whisk until smooth. Place into a fondue pot and serve with pieces of peanut brittle and pretzel rods. **Suggestion**: you can have your guests dip their own peanut brittle or pretzel rods, or you can dip a few and place on a plate near the fondue pot.

Individual Chocolate Peppermint Coffee (1 Cup of Coffee)

1. 1 Ounce Kahlua
2. 2/3 Cup Hot Black Coffee
3. Sweetener To Taste
4. Peppermint Whipping Cream (by Land O Lake)

Pour Kahlua into a cup of hot coffee. Add sweetener to the coffee if you like. Top with a squirt of peppermint whipping cream. **Serving Idea**: Use a peppermint stick for a stir.

New Year's Day Shopping List

Produce

___ 2 Tablespoons Green Onions
___ 2 Tablespoons Celery
___ 1 Medium Red Bell Pepper
___ 1/2 Medium White Onion
___ 1 Small Head Cabbage
___ 1 Lemon (for lemon peel)
___ 1 Cup Green Grapes

Meat

___ 1 Package (4 oz.) Smoked Salmon
___ 10 Slices Bacon
___ 1 1/2 Pounds Deli Sliced Corned Beef

Pantry Items

___ 2 Cans (15.8 oz each) Black-eyed Peas
___ 1/4 Cup Vinaigrette Salad Dressing
___ 3/4 Cup Roasted Garlic Rice Vinegar
___ 3/4 Cup Powdered Sugar
___ 2 Jars (24 oz. each) Del Monte Tropical Fruit
___ 1/2 Cup Walnut Pieces
___ 1 Cup Chopped Pecans
___ 2 Tablespoons Creamy Poppy Seed Salad Dressing
___ 1/2 Cup Dijon Mustard
___ 1 Box (10.25 oz.) Moist Deluxe Spice Cake Mix
___ 1 Jar (18 oz.) Peanut Butter
___ 1 1/4 Cups Sugar
___ 1 Bag (10 oz.) Dark Chocolate Chunks (Nestle)
___ 1 Package (12 oz.) Semisweet Chocolate Morsels
___ 1 Box (8 oz.) Peanut Brittle
___ 1 Package (10 oz.) Pretzel Rods

Spices

___ 1 Teaspoon Ginger

Frozen and Refrigerated Products

___ 1 Package (8 oz.) Cream Cheese
___ 1 1/2 Cups Sharp Cheddar Cheese
___ 2 Containers (13.8 oz. each) Pillsbury Classic Pizza Crust
___ 2 Packages (8 oz. each) Sliced Baby Swiss Cheese
___ 4 Eggs
___ 3/4 Cup Butter
___ 1 Container (16.5 oz.) Refrigerator Sugar Cookie Dough
___ 3/4 Cup Whipping Cream
___ 1 Can Land O Lake Peppermint Whipping Cream

Miscellaneous

___ Assorted Crackers
___ 1 Bottle Kahlua
___ Coffee
___ Peppermint Sticks

Super Bowl Party

A fun party to throw for all the sports fans and even those who aren't. Everyone seems to get caught up in the spirit of rooting for a team. Because the game is the number one priority at this party, we put together recipes for your guests to nibble on any time during the game. Go Team Go!
Linda and Emily

Touchdown Mix

Chicken Chili Pom Poms

"Philly" Steak Squares

Tasty Cheese Football

Party Field Goals

Hot Cheese Punts

First Down Veggie Dip

Championship Brownies

Sodas, Beer and Wine

Touchdown Mix

1. 1 Package (9 3/4 oz.) Flamin' Hot Corn Chips
2. 1 Package (4 oz.) White Cheddar Popcorn
3. 4 Cups Mini Pretzels
4. 2 Cups Dry Roasted Peanuts

In a large serving bowl, mix above ingredients. **Serving Idea**: Serve in individual paper bags.

Chicken Chili Pom Poms

1. 1 1/4 Pounds Boneless, Skinless Chicken Breasts (about 4 breasts)
2. 12 Slices Bacon
3. 2/3 Cup Firmly Packed Brown Sugar
4. 1 Tablespoon Chili Powder

Preheat oven to 375 degrees. Cut chicken breasts into 1-inch cubes. Cut bacon slices into thirds. Wrap each chicken cube with a piece of bacon and secure with a toothpick. Stir together brown sugar and chili powder. Dredge wrapped chicken in brown sugar mixture. Coat a rack and broiler pan with nonstick cooking spray. Place wrapped chicken on rack and bake at 375 degrees for 30-35 minutes or until bacon is crisp and chicken is done.

"Philly" Steak Squares

1. 1 Package (16 oz.) Philly Beef Steak with Onions and Green Peppers
2. 1 Can (6 oz.) Portabella Mushroom Steak Sauce
3. 1 Package (8 oz.) Four Cheese Pizza Cheese
4. 1 Container (13.8 oz.) Refrigerated Pizza Crust

Preheat oven to 375 degrees. On stovetop, in large frying pan, cook Philly beef steak according to package directions, adding 1/2 of the mushroom sauce to the meat while it is cooking. Set aside. On a lightly sprayed 9x13-inch baking sheet, unroll the pizza crust and pat dough until it fills most of the cookie sheet. Spread the rest of the mushroom sauce over the top of the pizza crust. Spread the Philly steak mixture over the mushroom sauce and top with cheese. Bake at 375 degrees for 20 minutes. Remove from oven and cool slightly. Slice the pizza into squares. Serve warm.

Tasty Cheese Football

1. 1 Package (8 oz.) Cream Cheese (softened)
2. 1 Package (4 oz.) Pastrami (finely chopped)
3. 3 Tablespoons Green Onions (finely chopped)
4. 1/2 Cup Crushed Pecans

Mix cream cheese, pastrami and green onions. Shape into a football. Roll football in crushed pecans until it covers the mixture and looks like a brown football. Serve with assorted crackers.

Party Field Goals

1. **2 Pounds Frozen Cooked Meatballs**
2. **1 Tablespoon Prepared Mustard**
3. **1 Bottle (12 oz.) Chili Sauce**
4. **1 Jar (10 oz.) Jalapeno Jelly**

On stovetop or crock-pot, mix together chili sauce, jalapeno jelly and mustard. Carefully stir in meatballs. Simmer, stirring occasionally, 30-40 minutes or until meatballs are thoroughly heated. Keep warm in crock-pot or stovetop.

Hot Cheese Punts

1. **1 Package (8 oz.) Grated Sharp Cheddar Cheese**
2. **1 Pound Ground Hot Sausage**
3. **3 1/2 Cups Biscuit Mix**
4. **1 Can (4.5 oz.) Diced Green Chiles**

Preheat oven to 375 degrees. Mix above ingredients and roll into 1-inch balls. Place on lightly sprayed baking sheet. Bake at 375 degrees for 10-15 minutes.
Helpful Hint: These can be made ahead and frozen on a cookie sheet and then stored in a plastic bag until ready to thaw and bake.

First Down Veggie Dip

1. **1 Cup Sour Cream**
2. **1/4 Cup Chicken Wing Sauce**
3. **1/2 Cup Finely Chopped Celery**
4. **Assorted Fresh Vegetables**

In serving bowl, mix the first three ingredients and refrigerate until ready to serve. Wash and cut the assorted vegetables to serve with the dip.

Championship Brownies

1. **1 Box (19.8 oz.) Brownie Mix (baked according to package directions)**
2. **36 Caramels (unwrapped)**
3. **1/2 Cup Whipping Cream**
4. **1 Cup Pecan Pieces**

Bake brownies according to package directions, remove from oven and allow the brownies to cool for 15 minutes. While brownies are baking, combine caramels and cream in medium saucepan and cook over low heat until caramels are melted and the mixture is smooth, stirring occasionally. Add pecans and stir until the nuts are well coated. Remove from heat. Spread caramel pecan layer over baked brownies. Cool to room temperature. Cover and refrigerate until caramel is set, approximately 45 minutes.

Super Bowl Party Shopping List

Produce
- ___ 3 Tablespoons Green Onions
- ___ 1/2 Cup Celery
- ___ Assorted Fresh Vegetables for Dipping

Bread, Crackers, Chips
- ___ 1 Package (9 3/4 oz.) Flamin' Hot Corn Chips
- ___ 1 Package (4 oz.) White Cheddar Popcorn
- ___ 4 Cups Mini Pretzels
- ___ Assorted Crackers

Meat
- ___ 1 1/4 Pound Boneless, Skinless Chicken Breasts
- ___ 12 Slices Bacon
- ___ 1 Package (4 oz.) Pastrami
- ___ 2 Pounds Frozen Cooked Meatballs
- ___ 1 Pound Ground Hot Sausage

Pantry Items
- ___ 2 Cups Dry Roasted Peanuts
- ___ 2/3 Cup Brown Sugar
- ___ 1 Can (6 oz.) Portabella Mushroom Steak Sauce
- ___ 1/2 Cup Crushed Pecans plus 1 Cup Pecan Pieces
- ___ 1 Tablespoon Prepared Mustard
- ___ 1 Bottle (12 oz.) Chili Sauce
- ___ 1 Jar (10 oz.) Jalapeno Jelly
- ___ 3 1/2 Cups Biscuit Mix
- ___ 1 Can (4.5 oz.) Diced Green Chiles
- ___ 1 Box (19.8 oz.) Brownie Mix Plus Ingredients Listed On Box
- ___ 1 Package Kraft Caramels (36 caramels
- ___ 1/4 Cup Chicken Wing Sauce

Spices
- ___ 1 Tablespoon Chili Powder

Frozen and Refrigerated Products
- ___ 1 Package (16 oz.) Philly Beef Steak With Onions and Green Peppers
- ___ 1 Package (8 oz.) Four Cheese Pizza Cheese
- ___ 1 Container (13.8 oz.) Refrigerated Pizza Crust
- ___ 1 Package (8 oz.) Cream Cheese
- ___ 1 Package (8 oz.) Grated Sharp Cheddar Cheese
- ___ 1 Container (8 oz.) Sour Cream
- ___ 1/2 Cup Whipping Cream

Miscellaneous
- ___ Individual Paper Bags
- ___ Cooking Spray
- ___ Sodas, Beer and Wine

Valentine's Day

Valentine's Day is a special day to tell someone that we care for them and love them. We associate chocolate, hearts, flowers, chocolate, candlelight dinners, the color red and chocolate with this romantic day. Use this special day to show someone you care. Be Our Valentine!

Linda and Emily

Crab Bisque

Spinach and Dried Cranberry Salad

Beef Tenderloin with Sherried Mushrooms

Saucy Asparagus

Love Bread

Double Chocolate Trifle

Crab Bisque

1. 1 Jar (26 oz.) Tomato Basil Sauce
2. 2 Cups Half and Half
3. 1/3 Cup Cooking Sherry or white cooking wine
4. 1 Can (6 oz.) White Crab Meat (drained)

Puree tomato sauce in blender or food processor. Place in saucepan and add half and half. Heat on low. Measure 1/3 cup cooking sherry in bowl and add crabmeat. Let marinate for about 15 minutes. Immediately before serving, add crab/sherry mixture to soup and bring to a simmer. Serve hot. **Suggestion**: sprinkle with flavored toasted bread crumbs or croutons.

Spinach and Dried Cranberry Salad

1. 2 Bags (6 oz. each) Baby Spinach (torn into bite-size pieces)
2. 1/2 Medium Red Onion (sliced)
3. 1 Package (6 oz.) Dried Sweetened Cranberries
4. 1/2 Cup Feta Cheese

In salad bowl, combine above ingredients and toss. Use with Raspberry Vinaigrette Salad Dressing or your favorite vinaigrette salad dressing.

Beef Tenderloin With Sherried Mushrooms

1. **4-5 Pounds Whole Beef Tenderloin**
2. **1 Pound Fresh Mushrooms (cleaned and sliced)**
3. **1 Cup Cooking Sherry**
4. **1 Tablespoon Minced Garlic**

Preheat oven to 425 degrees. Trim and remove fat and silver membrane from outside of tenderloin. Cut loin in half so it will fit in a large skillet. Generously spray bottom of large skillet with cooking spray and pre-heat to medium high. Place both pieces of tenderloin in preheated skillet and sear meat (approximately 2-3 minutes per side) or until brown. Remove meat from skillet and place onto a foil lined baking pan. Pour any remaining liquid from skillet over meat. Place into oven onto middle rack and bake at 425 degrees for 10 minutes per pound or until internal temperature of meat thermometer reaches 135 degrees for medium rare. The thinner piece of meat will be for those who like their meat cooked more. Remove from oven, cover with foil, and let stand 10 minutes before carving.

While tenderloin is cooking, sauté garlic (approximately 1 minute) in large skillet sprayed with cooking spray. Reduce heat and add mushrooms and continue to cook, stirring frequently, for approximately 4 minutes. Add sherry to mushrooms and simmer for 5 minutes reducing some of the liquid. Turn skillet off and let sherried mushrooms sit until ready to reheat. Prior to serving, quickly reheat mushrooms and serve with the tenderloin.

Saucy Asparagus

1. **2 Pounds Asparagus (washed and tough larger ends removed)**
2. **1 Package (1.25 oz.) Hollandaise Sauce Mix (prepared according to package directions. We used the one that requires water.)**
3. **1/4 Cup Diced Roasted Red Peppers**
4. **2 Teaspoons Fresh Lemon Juice**

Add 3 tablespoons of water to a 9x13-inch microwave dish. Place asparagus in dish, thick stems facing center of dish, and cover with plastic wrap. Poke holes in wrap to vent. Microwave for 5 minutes or until crisp-tender. Drain. Prepare Hollandaise Sauce according to package directions. Add roasted red pepper and lemon juice to hollandaise sauce mix. Pour over asparagus and serve.

Love Bread

1. **2 Cans (11 oz. each) Refrigerated Crusty French Loaf**
2. **1/2 Stick Butter (melted)**
3. **1 Tablespoon Dried Dill**
4. **1/4 Cup Grated Parmesan Cheese**

Preheat oven to 350 degrees. Open bread dough and place on cookie sheet. Form loaves to make a large heart shaped ring. Slice ends of the bread roll at a diagonal where they join to make the heart shape more accurately. Make sure the seam side of the bread roll is down. Pinch ends of bread together where they join. With a serrated knife, slice bread 2/3 of the way through loaf, every 1 to 1 1/2 inches. Melt butter and add dill. Brush loaf with butter mixture. Sprinkle cheese evenly around the top of the bread loaves. Bake at 350 degrees for 25-30 minutes, or until bread is golden brown. Serve on a flat platter to show off the heart design.

Double Chocolate Trifle

1. **1 Box (19.8 oz.) Fudge Brownie Mix**
2. **2 Containers (22 oz. each) Prepared Chocolate Pudding**
3. **1 Container (12 oz.) Extra Creamy Cool Whip**
4. **1 Package (8 oz.) Heath English Toffee Bits**

Bake brownie mix according to package directions for cake-like brownies. Allow to completely cool. Divide brownies into thirds. Remove from pan and tear into bite-size pieces. Place a layer of brownies on the bottom of a trifle bowl, followed by a layer of pudding, cool whip and candy bits. Repeat layers twice, ending with candy. Cover with plastic wrap and refrigerate until ready to serve.

Valentine's Day Shopping List

Produce

__ 2 Bags (6 oz. each) Baby Spinach
__ 1/2 Medium Red Onion
__ 1 Pound Fresh Mushrooms
__ 2 Pounds Asparagus
__ 1 Lemon
__ 1 Tablespoon Minced Garlic

Meat

__ 1 Can (6 oz.) White Crab Meat
__ 4-5 Pounds Whole Beef Tenderloin

Pantry Items

__ 1 Jar (26 oz.) Tomato Basil Sauce
__ 1 Package (6 oz.) Dried Sweetened
　　 Cranberries
__ 1 1/3 Cup Cooking Sherry
__ 1 Package (1.25 oz.) Hollandaise Sauce Mix
　　 (made with water)
__ 1/4 Cup Diced Roasted Red Peppers
__ 1 Box (19.8 oz.) Box Fudge Brownie Mix
　　 Plus Ingredients Listed On Box
__ 2 Containers (22 oz.) Prepared Chocolate
　　 Pudding
__ 1 Package (8 oz.) Heath English Toffee Bits

Spices

__ 1 Tablespoon Dried Dill

Frozen and Refrigerated Products

__ 2 Cups Half and Half
__ 1/2 Cup Feta Cheese
__ 2 Cans (11 oz. each) Refrigerator Crusty
　　 French Loaf
__ 1/2 Stick Butter
__ 1/4 Cup Grated Parmesan Cheese
__ 1 Container (12 oz.) Extra Creamy Cool
　　 Whip

Miscellaneous

__ Bread Crumbs or Croutons
__ Raspberry Vinaigrette Salad Dressing or
　　 other Vinaigrette Salad Dressing

Easter

While this holiday has significant religious meaning, it's also a great time to celebrate the return of Spring. Our families often celebrate and these are some of our favorite traditional Easter recipes.

Linda and Emily

Deviled Eggs

Mango and Kiwi Salad

Chilled Tomato and Cucumber Salad

Glazed Orange Ham

Potato Bacon Casserole

Zesty Carrots

Cinnamon Butter Rolls

Angel Coconut Butter Cake

Deviled Eggs

1. **1 Dozen Eggs (hard boiled)**
2. **1/4 Cup Dill Pickle Relish**
3. **1/3 Cup Mayonnaise**
4. **2 Teaspoons Mustard**

Shell eggs, cut in half lengthwise, and remove yolks. In small mixing bowl, mash yolks, and mix dill pickle relish, mayonnaise and mustard. Fill centers of whites with yolk mixture. Cover and refrigerate until ready to serve. Makes 24 deviled eggs. **Helpful Hint**: The fresher the egg, the more difficult it is to peel.

Mango and Kiwi Salad

1. **1 Jar (24.5 oz.) Pineapple Chunks (drained)**
2. **2 Fresh Mangos (peeled and cubed)**
3. **3 Fresh Kiwi Fruit (peeled and sliced)**
4. **3 Tablespoons Raspberry Pecan Salad Dressing**

In serving bowl, combine and mix pineapple, mango and kiwi slices. Add Raspberry Pecan Salad Dressing. Chill until ready to serve.

Chilled Tomato and Cucumber Salad

1. **1 1/2 Pints Small Cherry Tomatoes (cut in half)**
2. **1 Large Burpless Cucumber (peeled)**
3. **1/2 Cup Bottled Ranch Salad Dressing**
4. **1 Tablespoon Rice Vinegar**

Cut peeled cucumber in half lengthwise and then slice into thin slices. In serving bowl, combine tomatoes and cucumbers. In separate bowl, mix ranch dressing with rice vinegar. Pour over tomatoes and cucumbers. Season to taste. Chill until ready to serve.

Glazed Orange Ham

1. **1 Fully Cooked Spiral Cut Ham (6-8 Pounds)**
2. **1/3 Cup Mustard**
3. **1/2 Cup Firmly Packed Brown Sugar**
4. **1 Jar (18 oz.) Orange Marmalade**

Preheat oven to 350 degrees. Wrap the ham completely in foil and heat cut side down in shallow pan for 1 hour at 350 degrees. While ham is heating, combine the mustard, brown sugar and orange marmalade. Remove the ham from oven and remove foil. Increase oven temperature to 425 degrees and place ham, fat side up, back into pan. Brush and spoon orange marmalade sauce all over the ham. Return to oven and bake at 425 degrees for 10 minutes. Remove from oven and serve.

Potato Bacon Casserole

1. 1 Package (28 oz.) Frozen Potatoes O'Brien
2. 6 Slices Peppered Bacon
3. 2 Cups Cheddar Cheese (grated)
4. 1 Cup Sour Cream

Preheat oven to 350 degrees. In a large skillet, fry bacon over medium heat, turning once. When bacon is crisp, remove from skillet and drain on a paper towel. Crumble bacon and set aside. Retain about 3 tablespoons of bacon grease in skillet and add frozen potatoes to the skillet. Turn heat to low and allow potatoes to cook for 10-12 minutes. Potatoes should be soft, but not browned, stir occasionally. Remove from heat and place into a large bowl. Add cheddar cheese, bacon, and sour cream. Mix well and place into a lightly sprayed casserole dish. Bake at 350 degrees for 1 hour.

Zesty Carrots

1. 3 Pounds Raw Carrots (peeled and sliced 1-inch diagonally)
2. 1 Bottle (11 oz.) GourMayo Wasabi Horseradish
3. 1/2 Medium Onion (grated)
4. 1 Bag (6 oz.) Buttery Garlic Croutons

Preheat oven to 375 degrees. Cook carrots in seasoned boiling water, until crisp tender, approximately 10 minutes. Drain, reserving 1/2 cup liquid. Place carrots in a 8x8-inch baking dish. Combine reserved liquid, grated onion and mayonnaise and spread over carrots. Top with croutons. Bake at 375 degrees for 15 minutes. Do not over bake.

Cinnamon Butter Rolls

1. **18 Rhodes Frozen Rolls**
2. **1/2 Stick Butter (melted)**
3 **2 Tablespoons Cinnamon/Sugar**
4. **1/4 Teaspoon Nutmeg**

Thaw rolls according to package directions. When thawed and risen, place on baking sheet. Preheat oven to 350 degrees. In sauce pan, melt butter. Combine cinnamon/sugar, nutmeg and melted butter. Brush tops of rolls and bake at 350 degrees for 15-20 minutes. Remove rolls from baking sheet while they are still hot so they won't stick to the pan.

Angel Coconut Butter Cake

1. **1 Box (18.25 oz.) Butter Recipe Golden Cake Mix**
2. **2 Cups Sweetened Angel Flake Coconut**
3. **2 Cups Sour Cream**
4. **1 Container (8 oz.) Cool Whip**

Bake cake mix according to package directions using two cake pans. Allow to cool completely. When cool, split layers to make four layers. In bowl, mix the coconut and sour cream. Set aside 1 cup of this mixture to use in the frosting. Use the remainder to frost in between layers of cake. Fold the 1 cup of reserved coconut mixture into the Cool Whip. Frost top and sides of the cake. Cover and refrigerate until ready to serve. **Helpful Hint**: Dental floss is a great tool for cutting through a layered cake. Simply take a long piece of dental floss, pull it taut and saw through.

Easter Shopping List

Produce

- __ 2 Mangos
- __ 3 Kiwis
- __ 1 1/2 Pints Small Cherry Tomatoes
- __ 1 Large Burpless Cucumber
- __ 3 Pounds Carrots
- __ 1/2 Medium Onion

Bread, Crackers, Chips

- __ 1 Bag (6 oz.) Buttery Garlic Croutons

Meat

- __ 1 (6-8 Pounds) Fully Cooked Spiral Cut Ham
- __ 6 Slices Peppered Bacon

Pantry Items

- __ 1/4 Cup Dill Pickle Relish
- __ 1/3 Cup Mayonnaise
- __ 2 Teaspoon Mustard + 1/3 Cup
- __ 1 Jar (24 oz.) Pineapple Chunks
- __ 3 Tablespoons Raspberry Pecan Salad Dressing
- __ 1/2 Cup Brown Sugar
- __ 1 Tablespoon Rice Vinegar
- __ 1 Jar (18 oz.) Orange Marmalade
- __ 2 Cups Sweetened Flaked Coconut
- __ 1 Box (18.25 oz.) Butter Recipe Golden Cake Mix Plus Ingredients Listed On Box
- __ 1/2 Cup Ranch Salad Dressing
- __ 1 Bottle (11 oz.) GourMayo Wasabi Horseradish

Spices

- __ 2 Tablespoons Cinnamon/Sugar
- __ 1/4 Teaspoon Nutmeg

Frozen and Refrigerated Products

- __ 1 Dozen Eggs
- __ 1 Package (28 oz.) Frozen Potatoes O'Brien
- __ 3 Cups Sour Cream
- __ 18 Rhodes Frozen Rolls
- __ 1/2 Stick Butter
- __ 1 Container (8 oz.) Cool Whip
- __ 2 Cups Cheddar Cheese (grated)

Miscellaneous

- __ Cooking Spray

Ladies' Luncheon/Mother's Day

We serve this luncheon as a celebration of moms and girlfriends. Although the second week of May is the time we honor Moms, any lady would enjoy this Springtime Luncheon. Colorful springtime flowers, lace, frills can add that feminine flair.

Linda and Emily

Ladies Mimosa With Strawberries

Southern Mint Tea

Chicken Salad

Shrimp Salad

Colorful Spinach Salad

Sunny Cheese Bread Roses

Strawberries and Cream Dessert

Ladies Mimosa With Strawberries

1. **1 Bottle of Champagne (chilled)**
2. **1 Carton of Orange Juice**
3. **Fresh Strawberries (sliced)**
4. **Sugar**

For each serving, fill half of the champagne glass with chilled champagne. Fill the remainder of the glass with orange juice and gently stir. Dip each strawberry slice in sugar. Place strawberry slice on the rim of each glass.

Southern Mint Tea

1. **2 Cups Water Plus Additional Water to Make 1 Gallon Tea**
2. **2 Bags Plantation Mint Tea**
3. **2 Family Size Bags of Regular Tea**
4. **2/3 Cup Sugar**

In microwave, heat 2 cups water for about 5 minutes on high. Remove from microwave and add the mint tea and regular tea bags. Allow to steep for 10 minutes. Place 3 quarts of cold water in a one gallon pitcher. Add sugar and concentrated tea to the pitcher. Stir. Add additional water to completely fill pitcher. Cover and refrigerate until ready to serve. **Serving Idea**: Garnish with fresh mint leaves.

Chicken Salad

1. 3 1/2 Cups Cooked Diced Chicken
2. 2/3 Cup Sweetened Dried Cranberries (chopped)
3. 2/3 Cup Mayonnaise
4. 1/2 Cup Almonds (sliced)

Place diced chicken in mixing bowl. Add mayonnaise and cranberries and stir until well combined. Add almond slices and stir. Cover mixture and refrigerate until ready to serve. **Suggestion**: Place in a mound on plate and garnish with cantaloupe slice.

Shrimp Salad

1. 1 Pound Medium Fresh Cooked Shrimp (peeled and deveined)
2. 1/2 Green Pepper (finely chopped)
3. 2 Green Onions (finely chopped)
4. 1/4 Cup Lime and Garlic Salsa

Combine above ingredients, stir and marinate overnight. **Suggestion**: Place on a bed of lettuce or serve with a large slice of avocado.

Colorful Spinach Salad

1. **1 Pound Fresh Spinach (washed and dried)**
2. **1/2 Small Head Purple Cabbage**
3. **1 Package (7 oz.) Dried Tropical Fruit Mix**
4. **1 Package (2 oz.) Pecan Pieces**

In serving bowl, tear the spinach and cabbage into bite-sized pieces. Add the fruit mix and pecan pieces. Toss. Serve with a Spinach Vinaigrette Salad Dressing.

Sunny Cheese Bread "Roses"

1. **2 Cans (8 oz. each) Refrigerated Crescent Rolls**
2. **2 Tablespoons Butter (melted)**
3. **1/2 Cup Sharp Cheddar Cheese (finely grated)**
4. **Sesame Seeds**

Preheat oven to 350 degrees. On waxed paper sprayed with cooking spray, unroll each crescent roll (don't separate into triangles). Each can makes 1 large rectangle. You should now have two large rectangles. Sprinkle each surface with 1/4 cup grated cheese. Starting at long side, roll each dough rectangle into long slender cylinder. Cut each cylinder into 12 equal slices. Place slices in lightly sprayed mini muffin tin, cut side up. Score top of each roll with a sharp knife in an "X". Brush with melted butter and sprinkle with sesame seeds. Bake at 350 degrees for 16-18 minutes.

Strawberries and Cream Dessert

1. **2 Quarts Fresh Strawberries (washed, dried and sliced)**
2. **1/4 Cup Sugar**
3. **1/2 Cup Cream de Cocoa**
4. **1 Can (14 oz.) Land O Lake Creamy Whipped Cream (sprayed from can)**

To make a thick cream, in a large mixing bowl, spray whipped cream from the container to fill the bowl. Add sugar and Cream de Cocoa and stir to the consistency of a thick cream (not as thick as cool whip). If needed more whipped cream can be added. Gently fold the strawberries into the cream. Serve in individual parfait glasses or small bowls.

Ladies Luncheon/Mother's Day Shopping List

Produce
___ 2 Quarts Fresh Strawberries
___ Fresh Strawberries (Mimosas)
___ 2 Green Onions
___ 1 Pound Fresh Spinach
___ 1/2 Small Head Purple Cabbage
___ 1/2 Green Pepper

Meat
___ 4-5 Frozen, Boneless, Skinless Chicken
     Breasts Halves
___ 1 Pound Medium Cooked Shrimp

Pantry Items
___ Sugar
___ Plantation Mint Tea Bags
___ Family Size Tea Bags
___ 2/3 Cup Sweetened Dried Cranberries
___ 2/3 Cup Mayonnaise
___ 1/2 Cup Sliced Almonds
___ 1/4 Cup Lime and Garlic Salsa
___ 1 Package (7 oz.) Dried Tropical Fruit Mix
___ 1 Package (2 oz.) Pecan Pieces

Spices
___ Sesame Seeds

Frozen and Refrigerated Products
___ Orange Juice (Mimosa)
___ 2 Cans (8 oz. each) Refrigerated Crescent
     Rolls
___ 2 Tablespoons Butter
___ 1/2 Cup Sharp Cheddar Cheese
___ 1 Can (14 oz.) Land O Lake Creamy
     Whipped Cream

Miscellaneous
___ Champagne (Mimosa)
___ 1/2 Cup Cream de Cocoa

Father's Day

A day we like to honor our fathers for all the great love and strength they have shown us throughout our lives. Invite the family over and celebrate your father, or all the father's at the table. Tell your Dad how much you love him, and show him with these down home comfort food recipes. Thanks Dad!

Linda and Emily

Chilled Buffalo Bleu Cheese Salad

Beef Roast With Vegetables

Basil Garlic Mashed Potatoes

Southern Style Green Beans

Rancher's Rolls

Butter Pecan Pie

Chilled Buffalo Bleu Cheese Salad

1. **2 Heads of Iceberg Lettuce (each cut into quarters)**
2. **2 Large Tomatoes (diced)**
3. **1 Bottle Buffalo Bleu Cheese Salad Dressing**
4. **1 Container (8 oz.) Bleu Cheese Crumbles**

Immediately before serving, place the eight quartered lettuce wedges in freezer for about 1-2 minutes to chill. Important: Do not leave lettuce longer or it will freeze. Remove from freezer and sprinkle each wedge with diced tomatoes. Drizzle with Buffalo Bleu Cheese Salad Dressing and sprinkle with Bleu Cheese crumbles.

Beef Roast With Vegetables

1. **5 Pounds Boneless Beef Shoulder Roast**
2. **2 Pounds Baby Carrots**
3. **2 Large White Onions (peeled and sliced)**
4. **1 Package (1 oz.) Dry Au Jus Mix**

Preheat oven to 350 degrees. Mix dry Au Jus Mix with 2 cups water. In frying pan sprayed with cooking spray, brown roast on both sides. Take out of frying pan and place roast into a roasting pan. Place carrots and onions around roast. Pour Au Jus Mix over roast. Cover and bake for 3 1/2 hours at 350 degrees. **Suggestion**: Left over Au Jus can be used for gravy over the potatoes.

Basil Garlic Mashed Potatoes

1. **5 Pounds of Red Potatoes (peeled and cut into small pieces)**
2. **1 Container (8 oz.) Rondele Garlic and Herb Gourmet Spreadable Cheese**
3. **3/4 Cup Milk (heated)**
4. **3 Tablespoons Fresh Basil (chopped)**

Cover potatoes with water and bring to a boil. Boil potatoes approximately 15 minutes or until tender. Drain and mash with electric mixer. Add spreadable cheese and milk and continue mixing. Fold in fresh basil. Keep warm until ready to serve.

Southern Style Green Beans

1. **3 Cans (14 1/2 oz. each) Whole Green Beans**
2. **8 Slices Center Cut Bacon (cooked and crumbled)**
3. **1 Large Onion (chopped)**
4. **1/3 Cup White Vinegar**

On stovetop in large skillet, cook bacon until brown and crisp. Remove, drain and crumble bacon. Pour off all but 2 tablespoons drippings (leave in pan). Add onion to skillet along with vinegar and simmer for approximately 1 minute. Add drained green beans and mix with vinegar mixture. Season to taste. Add crumbled bacon and cook over low heat until warm.

Rancher's Rolls

1. **18 Rhodes Frozen Rolls (thawed according to package directions)**
2. **1 Stick Unsalted Butter (melted)**
3. **1 Tablespoon Dry Ranch Dressing Mix**
4. **2 Tablespoons Fresh Parsley**

Preheat oven to 350 degrees. In small bowl, mix butter, ranch dressing mix and parsley. After rolls are thawed and before they have risen, cut each roll into 3 pieces and dip into butter mixture. Place into a lightly sprayed tube or bundt pan. When all rolls have been placed in pan, cover top with plastic wrap that has been sprayed with cooking spray. This will prevent tops of rolls from sticking to plastic wrap. Place in warm area of the kitchen and allow rolls to rise, approximately 3-4 hours or until doubled in size. Bake at 350 degrees for 15-20 minutes until golden brown.

Butter Pecan Pie   Chocolate Crumb Pie Shell

1. **1/2 Gallon Butter Pecan Ice Cream**
2. **3 Tablespoons Hershey's Classic Caramel Topping**
3. **3 Tablespoons Heath Shell Chocolate with Toffee Bits**
4. **1 Can Whipped Heavy Cream (Land O Lakes)**

Soften ice cream at room temperature. Place one-half of the softened ice cream into chocolate crumb pie shell. Drizzle caramel topping over ice cream. Place other half of the ice cream on top of caramel. Drizzle chocolate over ice cream and cover. Put back in freezer until ready to serve. Five minutes before you are ready to serve pie, remove from freezer. Slice into serving pieces and top each piece with whipped cream.

Father's Day Shopping List

Produce
- __ 2 Pounds Baby Carrots
- __ 3 Large White Onions
- __ 5 Pounds Red Potatoes
- __ 3 Tablespoons Fresh Basil
- __ 2 Heads Iceberg Lettuce
- __ 2 Large Tomatoes
- __ 2 Tablespoons Fresh Parsley

Meat
- __ 5 Pounds Boneless Beef Shoulder Roast
- __ 8 Slices Center Cut Bacon

Pantry Items
- __ 1 Package (1 oz.) Dry Au Jus Mix
- __ 3 Cans (14.5 oz. each) Whole Green Beans
- __ 1/3 Cup White Vinegar
- __ 1 Bottle Buffalo Bleu Cheese Salad Dressing
- __ 1 Tablespoon Dry Ranch Dressing Mix
- __ 3 Tablespoons Hershey's Classic Caramel Topping
- __ 3 Tablespoons Heath Shell Chocolate with Toffee Bits
- __ 1 Chocolate Crumb Pie Shell

Frozen and Refrigerated Products
- __ 1 Container (8 oz.) Rondele Garlic and Herb Gourmet Spreadable Cheese
- __ 3/4 Cup Milk
- __ 1 Container (8 oz.) Bleu Cheese Crumbles
- __ 18 Rhodes Frozen Rolls
- __ 1 Stick Unsalted Butter
- __ 1/2 Gallon Butter Pecan Ice Cream
- __ 1 Can Land O Lake Creamy Whipped Cream

Miscellaneous
- __ Cooking Spray

Memorial Day

We honor and pay respect to our fallen soldiers by flying our flags at half-staff. This day is also considered the unofficial start of summer. Try these easy cool summer day dishes for this holiday.
Linda and Emily

Red and White Pinwheels

Pineapple Coconut Fruit Dip

Baby Back BBQ Pork Ribs

Potato Salad

Twice Baked Beans

Carrot Salad

Lemonade Pudding

Red and White Pinwheels

1. Spinach or Tomato Flour Tortillas (we used three 10-inch tortillas)
2. 1 Package (8 oz.) Cream Cheese (soften)
3. 1/2 to 1 Can (4 oz.) Chopped Green Chiles (drained)
4 1 Jar (4 oz.) Chopped Red Pimentos (drained)

Beat cream cheese until smooth. Add green chiles and red pimentos and mix to combine. Spread mixture on surface of each tortilla to the edge. Roll tortilla tightly and place in airtight container and refrigerate at least two hours. Slice each roll into 1-inch slices forming a pinwheel. Arrange on platter to serve.

Pineapple Coconut Fruit Dip

1. 1 Can (8 oz.) Crushed Pineapple (undrained)
2. 1 Package (3 1/2 oz.) Instant Coconut Pudding Mix
3. 3/4 Cup Milk
4. 1/2 Cup Sour Cream

In food processor, add crushed pineapple, coconut pudding mix, milk and sour cream. Process for at least 30 seconds. Pour into serving bowl and refrigerate for 2 hours or overnight. This will allow flavors to blend. Serve with assortment of fresh fruit. **Serving Idea**: Slice a fresh pineapple in half lengthwise and hollow out inside of pineapple to use as a fresh fruit bowl. Place some of the fresh pineapple around the dip along with the other fruit.

Baby Back BBQ Pork Ribs

1. **4-5 Pounds Baby Back Ribs (2 racks)**
2. **1 Can Beer**
3. **1/2 Cup Thai Peanut Sauce**
4. **1 Cup BBQ Sauce**

Preheat oven to 300 degrees. Form circle with each rack of ribs so that they stand up. Place ribs on rack and broiler pan, so that any fat can drip away. Place on lower rack in oven and bake for approximately 4 hours. While ribs are cooking, mix together beer, peanut sauce and BBQ sauce. Divide sauce into two separate bowls, one for basting ribs and the other to heat and serve as extra sauce with the ribs. Baste ribs every 30-45 minutes. Cover ribs for the last hour so that ribs do not dry out. Meat should fall away from bones. Serve with extra sauce.

Potato Salad

1. **3 Pounds Red New Potatoes**
2. **1/3 Cup Cider Vinegar**
3. **2/3 Cup Mayonnaise**
4. **2/3 Cup Green Onions (sliced)**

In saucepan, cover potatoes with water and bring to a boil. Once potatoes boil, cover and reduce heat to medium low, simmering for 10 to15 minutes. Potatoes should be fork tender. Drain and cool slightly. Cut potatoes into quarters or smaller; and while still warm, stir in vinegar. Marinate in vinegar for 30 minutes, stirring occasionally. Drain excess vinegar off and add mayonnaise and green onions. Refrigerate. **Suggestion**: Can be made a day ahead.

Twice Baked Beans

1. **2 Cans (28 oz. each) Baked Beans with Bacon and Brown Sugar**
2. **6 Slices of Peppered Bacon (cut into 1-inch pieces)**
3. **1 Teaspoon Dry Mustard**
4. **1/2 Cup Ketchup**

Preheat oven to 350 degrees. Fry bacon until crisp, drain and break into pieces. Place beans, ketchup and mustard in crock-pot or baking dish. Stir to combine. Add bacon and toss to distribute. In oven, bake at 350 degrees for 30-45 minutes or until heated through. In crock-pot, cook on low for 3-4 hours.

Carrot Salad

1. **2 Pounds Whole Carrots (washed, peeled, grated)**
2. **1 Can (8 oz.) Pineapple Tidbits (drained and cut in half)**
3. **1/2 Cup Chopped Pecans**
4. **2/3 Cup Mayonnaise With Lime Juice**

Combine grated carrots, pineapple tidbits and pecans. Toss with mayo dressing. Cover and refrigerate until ready to serve.

Lemonade Pudding

1. 1 Can (6 oz.) Frozen Lemonade (thawed)
2. 1 Can (14 oz.) Sweetened Condensed Milk
3. 1 Carton (8 oz.) Cool Whip
4. 1 Package (14 oz.) Mother's Iced Lemonade Cookies

Crush cookies (about 24) into crumbs and divide crumbs into thirds. In a 8x8-inch baking dish, sprinkle 1/3 crumbs in bottom of dish. In mixing bowl, combine milk, cool whip and lemonade together. Spread 1/2 cup lemonade mixture on top of cookie crumbs. Sprinkle another layer of crumbs and then the remainder of lemonade mixture. Top with remaining third of crumbs. Refrigerate at least one hour or until firm.

Memorial Day Shopping List

Produce
- __ 3 Pounds Red New Potatoes
- __ 2/3 Cup Green Onions
- __ 2 Pounds Whole Carrots

Bread, Crackers, Chips
- __ Spinach or Tomato Flour Tortillas

Meat
- __ 4-5 Pounds Baby Back Ribs (2 racks)
- __ 6 Slices of Peppered Bacon

Pantry Items
- __ 1 Can (4 oz.) Chopped Green Chiles
- __ 1 Jar (4 oz.) Chopped Red Pimentos
- __ 1/2 Cup Thai Peanut Sauce
- __ 1 Cup BBQ Sauce
- __ 1/3 Cup Cider Vinegar
- __ 2/3 Cup Mayonnaise with Lime Juice
- __ 2/3 Cup Mayonnaise
- __ 2 Cans (28 oz. each) Baked Beans with Bacon and Brown Sugar
- __ 1/2 Cup Ketchup
- __ 1 Can (8 oz.) Pineapple Tidbits
- __ 1/2 Cup Chopped Pecans
- __ 1 Can (14 oz.) Sweetened Condensed Milk
- __ 1 Package (14 oz.) Mother's Iced Lemonade Cookies
- __ 1 Can (8 oz.) Crushed Pineapple
- __ 1 Package (3 1/2 oz.) Instant Coconut Pudding Mix

Spices
- __ 1 Teaspoon Dry Mustard

Frozen and Refrigerated Products
- __ 1 Package (8 oz.) Cream Cheese
- __ 1 Can (6 oz.) Frozen Lemonade
- __ 1 Carton (8 oz.) Cool Whip
- __ 3/4 Cup Milk
- __ 1/2 Cup Sour Cream

Miscellaneous
- __ 1 Can Beer

Fourth of July

Celebrate this fun and joyous holiday, Independence Day, with a backyard get together! Enjoy these easy blowout recipes with your fireworks. Kaboom!

Linda and Emily

Shrimp Skewer Sparklers

Spring Mix Salad

Firecracker Chicken

Melon Explosion

Corn on the Cob with Sizzle Butter

Explosive Broccoli Crowns

Strawberry Dessert

Shrimp Skewer Sparklers

1. **2 Pounds Medium Fresh Cooked Shrimp**
2. **1 Fresh Pineapple (cut into chunks)**
3. **1 Bag (12 oz.) Cherry Tomatoes**
4. **1 Bottle Sesame Ginger Salad Dressing (Paul Newman)**

If using wooden skewers, remember to soak in water before putting the food on them. This will prevent them from burning when you broil. Alternate and arrange shrimp, pineapple chunks, and cherry tomatoes on skewers. Place in casserole dish and pour salad dressing over the skewers to marinate. Cover with plastic wrap and refrigerate until ready to broil. Remove from refrigerator, place on baking sheet and brush with dressing from the casserole dish. Broil approximately 2 minutes per side - remember the shrimp is already cooked. **Suggestion**: These shrimp skewers are also good grilled.

Spring Mix Salad

1. **2 Bags (5 oz. each) Spring Mix Salad Greens**
2. **1 Large Hass Avocado (peeled, halved and sliced)**
3. **1 Bag (12 oz.) Cherry Tomatoes (halved)**
4. **1 Can (6 oz.) Small Pitted Black Olives (drained)**

In serving bowl, combine above ingredients. Cover and refrigerate until ready to serve. Serve or toss with your favorite salad dressing. **Helpful Hint**: Slice avocado in half and twist each half apart; remove seed. Using a large tablespoon, gently scoop avocado half out of peel.

Firecracker Chicken

1. **8 Boneless Skinless Chicken Breast Halves**
2. **2 Large Eggs plus 2 Tablespoons Water**
3. **1 Bag (13.25 oz.) Chile Limon Potato Chips (finely crushed)**
4. **1 Package (8 oz.) Monterrey Pepper Jack Cheese (cut into 8 slices, lengthwise)**

Preheat oven to 350 degrees. Remove as much visible fat from chicken as possible. Whisk eggs and water together until well combined. Dip chicken breast in egg mixture and then into crushed potato chips. Place on foil that has been lightly sprayed with cooking spray. Bake at 350 degrees for 40 minutes. Remove from oven and place cheese slices on top of each chicken breast. Return to oven for about 5 minutes or until cheese is melted.

Melon Explosion

1. **1 Small Seedless Watermelon**
2. **1 Cantaloupe**
3. **1 Honey Dew Melon**
4. **10 Limes (makes 2/3 cup fresh lime juice)**

Using a melon ball scoop, make balls with the insides of the watermelon, cantaloupe and honey dew. Place in bowl. Squeeze eight limes to make fresh lime juice, remove any seeds. Pour lime juice over melon balls and gently toss. Cover and refrigerate until chilled. When ready to serve, remove from the refrigerator, and use a slotted spoon to place melon balls into serving dish. Prior to serving, pour the juice from the remaining two limes over the melon balls. **Serving Idea**: Watermelon cavity can be used as a bowl.

Corn On The Cob With Sizzle Butter

1. **8 Ears Fresh Corn on Cob**
2. **1 Stick Butter (melted)**
3. **2 Fresh Jalapeno Peppers (washed and seeded)**
4. **1 Grated Lime Peel**

In blender, coarsely chop jalapenos; add butter and lime peel. Process until smooth and place into a small serving bowl. Boil corn in salted water for approximately 8 minutes. Drain and serve with jalapeno lime butter. **Suggestion**: The jalapeno lime butter can be made a day ahead, refrigerated and brought to room temperature before serving.

Explosive Broccoli Crowns

1. **2 Pounds Fresh Broccoli Crowns (cut in bite-size pieces)**
2. **1 Cup Caesar Ranch Flavored Gour Mayo**
3. **1 Tablespoon Roasted Garlic and Bell Pepper Seasoning**
4. **1 Cup Sharp Cheddar Cheese (grated)**

Wash and remove all tough stems from broccoli and cut into bite–size pieces. Mix mayo and seasoning. Toss with broccoli. Sprinkle grated cheese on top and refrigerate until ready to serve.

Strawberry Dessert

1. 1 (18.25 oz.) Strawberry Cake Mix
2. 1 Cup Cool Whip for Cake Mix and 3 Cups for Frosting
3. 3 Egg Whites
4. 1 Can (21 oz.) Strawberry Pie Filling

Preheat oven to 350 degrees. Combine cake mix, 1 cup cool whip and 1 cup water. Pour 1/2 of the batter into greased 9 x 13-inch cake pan. Open can of strawberry pie filling and with a fork, remove the whole strawberries, leaving the remaining filling to be used for the topping. Distribute the strawberries over the cake batter and cover with the remaining batter. Bake at 350 degrees for 35-40 minutes or until cake is done. Allow to cool. **Helpful Hint**: An 8 oz. tub of Cool Whip yields 3 cups of Cool Whip. A 12 oz. tub yields 4 1/2 cups; and a 16 oz. tub yields 6 1/2 cups of Cool Whip.

For frosting: add 1/4 cup of the pie filling to 3 cups of cool whip and combine. You can leave the cake in the pan and frost the top or remove from the pan and frost the top and sides. Place the remaining pie filling in a sandwich bag and cut off one small corner of the bag and "pipe" the glaze across the top of the frosting in any design that you prefer. Cover and refrigerate until ready to serve.

Fourth of July Shopping List

Produce

- 1 Fresh Pineapple
- 2 Bags (12 oz. each) Cherry Tomatoes
- 2 Bags (5 oz. each) Spring Mix Salad Greens
- 1 Large Hass Avocado
- 8 Ears Corn on Cob
- 2 Fresh Jalapeno Peppers
- 11 Limes
- 2 Pounds Fresh Broccoli Crowns
- 1 Small Seedless Watermelon
- 1 Cantaloupe
- 1 Honey Dew Melon

Bread, Crackers, Chips

- 1 Bag (13.25 oz.) Chile Limon Potato Chips

Meat

- 2 Pounds Medium Fresh Cooked Shrimp
- 8 Boneless, Skinless Chicken Breast Halves

Pantry Items

- 1 Bottle Sesame Ginger Salad Dressing (Paul Newman)
- 1 Can (6 oz.) Small Pitted Black Olives
- 1 Cup Caesar Ranch Flavored Gour Mayo
- 1 Box (18.25 oz.) Strawberry Cake Mix
- 1 Can (21 oz.) Strawberry Pie Filling

Spices

- 1 Tablespoon Roasted Garlic & Bell Pepper Seasoning

Frozen and Refrigerated Products

- 5 Large Eggs
- 1 Package (8 oz.) Monterrey Pepper Jack Cheese
- 1 Stick Butter
- 1 Cup Sharp Cheddar Cheese (grated)
- 1 Container (16 oz.) Cool Whip

Miscellaneous

- Cooking Spray

Labor Day

Labor Day, the first Monday in September, is a chance for one final fling before summer is over. This weekend should be a relaxed time to say farewell to summer's lazy days. Use this "labor less" menu so that you can sit back and enjoy the day too!

Linda and Emily

Summer Salsa

Beef Stick Stacks

Avocado Grapefruit Salad

Laborless Oven Smoked Brisket

Spicy Oven Fries

Fresh Basil, Tomato and Green Beans

Orange Angel Food Cake

Summer Salsa

1. 1 Can (28 oz.) Bush's Original Baked Beans
2. 1 Can (14.5 oz.) Diced Tomatoes With Jalapenos (drained)
3. 1 Cup Frozen Corn Kernels
4. 1 Cup Chopped Onion

Mix above ingredients in serving bowl. Chill in refrigerator. Serve with tortilla chips, Frito scoops, or sliced fresh baguette bread. **Suggestion**: Can be made a day ahead.

Beef Stick Stacks

1. 1 Pound Beef Stick Summer Sausage
2. 1 Jar (15 oz.) Whole Pearl Onions
3. 1 Container (8 oz.) Fresh Mozzarella Cheese Balls
4. 1 Jar (14 oz.) Mild Peppadews (whole sweet piquante peppers)

Unwrap and slice the beef stick into 1/4-inch slices. Stuff one peppedew with one cheese ball. If cheese balls are too large, cut in half. Place on top of slice of beef stick and top with one onion. Stick a toothpick down through center of onion and peppedew into sausage. Place on a large platter, cover and refrigerate until ready to serve.

Avocado Grapefruit Salad

1. 2 Jars (24 oz. each) Grapefruit Sections (well drained)
2. 3 Medium Avocados (peeled and chopped)
3. 1/2 Medium Red Onion (sliced thin)
4. 1/3 Cup Coleslaw Dressing

Cut grapefruit sections in bite-sized chunks. Cut thin slices of red onion into 1/2-inch lengths. In salad bowl, combine drained grapefruit sections, avocados and onions. Add coleslaw dressing and gently toss. Cover and refrigerate until ready to serve. **Suggestion**: Serve on a bed of lettuce.

Laborless Oven Smoked Brisket

1. 5-6 Pounds Beef Brisket (well trimmed)
2. 1/4 Cup Liquid Smoke
3. 1 Teaspoon Fajita Seasoning
4. 1/2 Cup Water

Preheat oven to 275 degrees. Combine liquid smoke, fajita seasoning and water. Place brisket on large sheet of heavy-duty foil in a shallow roasting pan. Pour sauce over brisket and turn until well coated. Seal foil tightly. Bake at 275 degrees for 5 to 7 hours, about 1-1/4 hour per pound. Remove from oven and allow to rest for 15 minutes before slicing. **Helpful Hint**: It is important to let the brisket sit a little while before carving. This allows the juices to retreat back into the meat.

Spicy Oven Fries

1. **2 Pounds Baking Potatoes**
2. **2 Tablespoons Olive Oil**
3. **2 Tablespoons Creole Seasoning**
4. **Parmesan Cheese (optional)**

Cut each potato lengthwise into 8 wedges. Combine olive oil and Creole seasoning in a zip-top plastic bag. Add potato wedges and seal bag. Shake to coat potatoes. Arrange potato wedges, skin side down, in a single layer on a baking sheet coated with nonfat cooking spray. Bake at 450 degrees for 20 minutes or until golden brown. Remove from oven and sprinkle with Parmesan cheese if desired.

Fresh Basil, Tomato and Green Beans

1. **2-3 Large Tomatoes (sliced into 8 slices)**
2. **1 Jar (18.7 oz.) Extra Fine Cooked Green Beans**
3. **1 Container (4 oz.) Feta Cheese**
4. **Fresh Basil (snipped)**

Refrigerate tomatoes and green beans so that they are chilled. Place tomato slices on serving platter. Divide the jar of green beans into 8 bundles. Place a bundle on top of each tomato slice. Sprinkle with fresh-snipped basil leaves and feta cheese. Refrigerate until ready to serve.

Orange Angel Food Cake

1. 1 Package (16 oz.) Angel Food Cake Mix
2. 2/3 Cup Frozen Orange Juice Concentrate (thawed)
3. 1 Container (12 oz.) Cool Whip
4. 1/4 Cup Plain Yogurt

Prepare Angel Food Cake as directed on package, but pour 1/3 cup of thawed orange juice into a 2-cup measure and add enough water for the mixture to equal the amount of water called for in the package directions. Bake according to directions. Cool completely. Combine Cool Whip, yogurt and remaining 1/3 cup orange juice concentrate. Frost top and sides of cake. Cover and refrigerate until ready to serve.

Labor Day Shopping List

Produce

- ___ 1 Onion (1 cup chopped)
- ___ 2 Pounds Baking Potatoes
- ___ 3 Medium Avocados
- ___ 1/2 Red Onion
- ___ 2-3 Large Tomatoes
- ___ Fresh Basil

Meat

- ___ 1 Pound Beef Stick Summer Sausage
- ___ 5-6 Pounds Trimmed Beef Brisket

Pantry Items

- ___ 1 Can (28 oz.) Bush's Original Baked Beans
- ___ 1 Can (14.5 oz.) Diced Tomatoes with Jalapenos
- ___ 1 Jar (15 oz.) Whole Pearl Onions
- ___ 1 Jar (14 oz.) Mild Peppadews (whole sweet piquante peppers)
- ___ 1/4 Cup Liquid Smoke
- ___ 2 Tablespoons Olive Oil
- ___ 1/3 Cup Coleslaw Dressing
- ___ 1 Jar (18.7 oz.) Extra Fine Cooked Green Beans
- ___ 1 Package Angel Food Cake Mix

Spices

- ___ 1 Teaspoon Fajita Seasoning
- ___ 2 Tablespoons Creole Seasoning

Frozen and Refrigerated Products

- ___ 1 Cup Frozen Corn Kernels
- ___ 1 Container (8 oz.) Fresh Mozzarella Cheese Balls
- ___ 2 Jars (24 oz. each) Grapefruit Sections
- ___ 1 Container (4 oz.) Feta Cheese
- ___ 1 Container (6 oz.) Frozen Orange Juice Concentrate
- ___ 1 Container (12 oz.) Cool Whip
- ___ 1/4 Cup Plain Yogurt

Miscellaneous

- ___ Parmesan Cheese (optional for Spicy Oven Fries)
- ___ Tortilla Chips, Frito Scoops or Sliced Fresh Baguette Bread

Autumn Harvest Dinner

Fall is one of our favorite times of the year. Gather your family and friends for a feast celebrating the abundance of your lives. These simple autumn recipes are perfect for the month of October.

Linda and Emily

Broccoli Cheese Herb Soup

Olive Cheese Ball Pumpkin Appetizers

Buffalo Pork Loin

Sherried Wild Rice

Yellow Squash Casserole

Harvest Bread Sticks

Apple Carrot Cake

Broccoli Cheese Herb Soup

1. 1 Package (24 oz.) Green Giant Broccoli And Three Cheese Sauce
2. 1 Jar (5 oz.) Old English Sharp Cheese Spread
3. 2 Cans (10 3/4 oz. each) Cream of Chicken with Herbs Soup (plus 2 soup cans of water)
4. 2 Cups Butter Flavored Croutons

Remove cheese sauce chips from the package of broccoli and place in large saucepan. Add Old English Cheese to saucepan with sauce chips and heat over low heat to melt, stirring occasionally. Leave the broccoli in package, allowing it to partially thaw for about 15 minutes. Place broccoli in food processor and process until broccoli is in very small chunks. When cheese is melted, add the two cans of soup and 2 cans of water and stir until well combined. Add the chopped broccoli and continue to heat until warm. Place soup in serving bowls and sprinkle with butter flavored croutons.

Olive Cheese Ball Pumpkin Appetizers

1. 16-18 Medium Pimento Stuffed Green Olives (drained and dried)
2. 1/2 Cup Flour
3. 1/4 Cup Butter (melted)
4. 1 Cup Finely Grated Extra Sharp Cheddar Cheese

Preheat oven to 400 degrees. In a small bowl, combine and mix well the flour, butter and cheddar cheese to form a smooth dough. Wrap a small amount of this mixture around each olive, about 1 teaspoon or enough to cover the olive. Place on a lightly sprayed cookie sheet and bake at 400 degrees for 12 minutes. **Suggestion**: You can make these olives ahead of time and refrigerate until you are ready to bake them.

Buffalo Pork Loin

1. **1 (4-5 Pounds) Pork Loin Roast**
2. **1 Cup Prepared Buffalo Wing Sauce**
3. **1 Tablespoon Garlic Powder**
4. **1 Teaspoon Celery Salt**

Place pork loin in gallon size zip lock bag with the wing sauce. Marinate overnight. Preheat oven to 400 degrees. Remove roast with sauce and place on foil in shallow oven pan. Mix garlic powder and celery salt and sprinkle over top of roast. Bake uncovered at 400 degrees for 30 minutes. Reduce heat to 325 degrees and bake for 1 to 1 1/2 hours or until loin reaches an internal temperature of 170 degrees. Baste several times while loin is baking. Remove from oven and allow loin to rest for 20 minutes, before slicing and serving.

Sherried Wild Rice

1. **2 Boxes (6 oz. each) Original Uncle Ben's Wild Rice**
2. **1 Cup Celery (chopped)**
3. **1 Cup White Onion (chopped)**
4. **3/4 Cup Dry Cooking Sherry**

Cook rice according to package directions, but reduce water to 4 cups. Set aside. In large frying pan sprayed with cooking spray, add 1/4 cup cooking sherry. Add onions and celery and cook until softened. Add cooked rice and remainder of sherry. Mix together well, heat and serve. **Suggestion**: Can be made a day ahead and reheated before serving.

Yellow Squash Casserole

1. **6 Medium Yellow Squash (peeled and sliced)**
2. **1 Cup Chopped Onion**
3. **1 Cup Velveeta Cheese (cut into 1/2 inch cubes)**
4. **1 Can (4 oz.) Chopped Green Chiles**

Preheat oven to 375 degrees. Boil squash and onion until tender. Drain well and mix with cheese and chiles. Pour into buttered baking dish. Bake at 375 degrees for 15 minutes or until bubbly.

Harvest Bread Sticks

1. **2 Boxes (10.6 oz. each) Refrigerator Bread Sticks**
2. **3 Tablespoons Butter (melted)**
3. **Sesame Seeds**
4. **Pumpkin Seeds**

Preheat oven to 375 degrees. Remove breadsticks according to container directions. Roll each bread stick in melted butter and place on cookie sheet. Sprinkle with sesame seeds and pumpkin seeds. Bake at 375 degrees for 10-14 minutes.

Apple Carrot Cake

1. 1 (18.25 oz.) Super Moist Carrot Cake Mix
2. 1 Cup Fresh Apples (peeled and chopped)
3. 1/2 Cup Chopped Pecans
4. 1 Can (16 oz.) Cream Cheese Frosting

Preheat oven to 350 degrees. Mix and prepare carrot cake mix according to package directions. Add apples and pecans to mixture. Pour mixture into two lightly sprayed 8-inch cake pans and bake at 350 degrees for 27-32 minutes. Allow to cool for 5 minutes before removing from pan. Allow to cool completely before frosting with cream cheese frosting. **Serving Idea**: Decorate frosted cake with pecans.

Autumn Harvest Shopping List

Produce
- ___ 1 Cup Celery (chopped)
- ___ 2 Cups White Onion
- ___ 6 Medium Yellow Squash
- ___ 1 Cup Fresh Apples

Breads, Crackers Chips
- ___ 2 Cups Butter Flavored Croutons

Meat
- ___ 4-5 Pounds Pork Loin Roast

Pantry Items
- ___ 2 Cans (10 3/4 oz. each) Cream of Chicken with Herbs Soup
- ___ 16-18 Medium Pimento Stuffed Green Olives
- ___ 1 Cup Buffalo Wing Sauce
- ___ 1 Jar (5 oz.) Old English Sharp Cheddar Cheese Spread
- ___ 1 Can (4 oz.) Chopped Green Chiles
- ___ 2 Boxes (6 oz. each) Original Uncle Bens Wild Rice
- ___ 3/4 Cup Dry Cooking Sherry
- ___ 1 Box (18.25 oz.) Super Moist Carrot Cake Plus Ingredients Listed On Box
- ___ 1/2 Cup Chopped Pecans
- ___ 1 Can (16 oz.) Cream Cheese Frosting
- ___ Flour

Spices
- ___ 1 Tablespoon Garlic Powder
- ___ 1 Teaspoon Celery Salt
- ___ Sesame Seeds
- ___ Pumpkin Seeds

Frozen and Refrigerated Products
- ___ 1 Package (24 oz.) Green Giant Broccoli & Three Cheese Sauce
- ___ 1/4 Cup Butter + 3 Tablespoons
- ___ 1 Cup Extra Sharp Cheddar Cheese (finely grated)
- ___ 1 Cup Velveeta Cheese
- ___ 2 Boxes (10.6 oz. each) Refrigerator Bread Sticks

Miscellaneous
- ___ Cooking Spray

Thanksgiving Dinner

Thanksgiving Day is always on the 4th Thursday in November. On this holiday, we celebrate and give thanks for the many blessings in our lives. We have put together a traditional Thanksgiving feast. Don't forget the pumpkin and pecan pies. Thank you!

Linda and Emily

Ambrosia Fruit Salad

Roasted Herbed Turkey With Gravy

Savory Mushroom Dressing

Orange Cranberry Relish

Creamy Mashed Potatoes

Sweet Potato Casserole

Parmesan Cauliflower

Traditional Relish Tray

Thanksgiving Rolls with Honey and Nut Butter

Pumpkin Pie

Pecan Pie

Ambrosia Fruit Salad

1. 2 Jars (24 oz. each) Mandarin Oranges (drained, retain 1/4 cup liquid)
2. 2 Jars (24.5 oz. each) Pineapple Chunks (drained)
3. 1 Cup Sweetened Flaked Coconut
4. 3 Bananas (sliced)

In serving bowl, add drained mandarin oranges, 1/4 cup of mandarin orange liquid, pineapple chunks, coconut and sliced bananas. Toss. Refrigerate until ready to serve. Serve with a slotted spoon.

Savory Mushroom Dressing

1. 2 Jars (6 oz. each) Sliced Mushrooms (retain fluid – about 1/2 cup each jar)
2. 2 Cans (14.5 oz. each) Chicken Broth
3. 1 Stick Butter
4. 1 Package (16 oz.) Pepperidge Farm Herbed Dressing

On stovetop in large pan, heat mushrooms, mushroom fluid, chicken broth and butter until butter is melted. Add dressing mix and toss until all the dressing is moist and heated through. Place into a 1 1/2 quart baking dish. Serve immediately.

Roasted Herbed Turkey With Gravy

1. 1 (14-15 Pounds) Turkey (thawed according to package directions)
2. 1 Stick Butter
3. 2 Tablespoons Salt Free McCormick All-Purpose Seasoning (blend of herbs & spices)
4. 6-8 Fresh Rosemary Springs (cut into 2-inch sprigs)

Preheat oven to 325 degrees. Remove turkey from packaging. Remove giblet packaging from both inside turkey cavity and neck cavity. Rinse turkey and pat dry. Place turkey in roasting pan. In small saucepan, melt butter and mix in seasoning. Baste turkey with 1/2 of the melted herb butter. Place rosemary sprigs on top of the turkey breasts and legs. Place into oven and cook for 3 1/2 hours, uncovered, or until turkey is done. After turkey has cooked for 1 1/2 hours, baste it again with the remaining herb butter and cover top of turkey with aluminum foil to prevent top from browning too much. Remove from oven and let turkey sit for 15 minutes before carving. **Suggestion**: We recommend using a meat thermometer to take the guess out of knowing when the turkey is done.

Turkey Gravy: Place the turkey neck and giblets that you removed from the turkey cavities into a medium saucepan with 4 cups of salted water. Simmer over low heat for 1 1/2 to 2 hours to reduce the liquid down to about 2 cups. Remove neck and giblets; strain broth and return broth to saucepan. After removing turkey from oven, pour turkey drippings that are on the bottom of the roasting pan through a strainer and add 1 cup of these strained drippings to the broth. Whisk together 1/3 cup flour into 1 cup COLD water and stir until there are no lumps. Bring broth and drippings to a simmer and add the flour and water mixture. Continue cooking and stirring until mixture returns to a simmer. Simmer for 3-5 minutes. Add pepper to taste.

Orange Cranberry Relish

1. 1 Bag (12 oz) Fresh Cranberries
2. 1 Jar (12 oz.) Orange Marmalade
3. 1/2 Cup Pecan Pieces
4. 1 Cup Sugar (dissolved in 1 cup water)

On stovetop simmer cranberries in 1-cup sugar and 1-cup water until the cranberries pop. Once they have popped remove from heat and mix in the orange marmalade and pecan pieces. Place into serving bowl and chill overnight or until ready to serve.

Creamy Mashed Potatoes

1. 5 Pounds Potatoes
2. 1 Package (4 oz.) Cream Cheese (softened)
3. 1 Cup Prepared Dill Dip with Real Sour Cream
4. 1 Cup Milk (heated)

Peel, quarter, and rinse potatoes. On stovetop, cook potatoes in boiling water until fork tender, soft but not mushy. Drain and place into large mixing bowl. Season to taste and add cream cheese, dill dip and milk. With electric mixer, beat until a creamy consistency. Place into casserole dish and serve. **Serving Idea**: Potatoes can be made ahead and reheated in the oven, covered, at 350 degrees for 30 minutes.

Sweet Potato Casserole

1. **2 Cans (29 oz. each) Sweet Potatoes (drained, reserve 1/4 cup liquid)**
2. **2 Tablespoons Pumpkin Pie Spice Mix**
3. **1 Cup Pecan Pieces**
4. **1 Bag (10 oz.) Toasted Coconut Marshmallows**

Preheat oven to 350 degrees. In large bowl with electric mixer, mix potatoes and pumpkin spice mix together. Place into a lightly sprayed 9x13-inch casserole. Sprinkle pecan pieces on top of potatoes. Cut each toasted coconut marshmallow in half and press onto top of the sweet potato and pecans. Use entire bag, marshmallows should be touching each other. Bake at 350 degrees for 20 minutes or until heated through. Watch closely to make certain marshmallows don't burn.

Parmesan Cauliflower

1. **2 Heads of Cauliflower**
2. **1 Cup of Freshly Grated Parmesan Cheese**
3. **1/3 Cup Mayonnaise**
4. **2 Teaspoons Vegetable Supreme Seasoning (plus additional for top)**

Wash cauliflower, remove stalks and cut into flowerets. Steam cauliflower until crisp tender. Combine mayonnaise, Parmesan cheese and 2 teaspoons vegetable seasoning. Place cooked cauliflower in large bowl and toss with mayonnaise/cheese mixture until all pieces are well coated. Place into microwave proof 1 1/2 quart casserole. Sprinkle top with vegetable seasoning. Cover and set aside. Immediately before serving, heat in microwave for 3 minutes or until warmed through.

Traditional Relish Tray Suggestions

Choose your favorites from below:

1. **Banana Peppers Stuffed With Cream Cheese.**
2. **Cherry Tomatoes Stuffed With Prepared Crab Dip**
3. **Celery Stuffed With Prepared Pimento Cheese**
4. **Sweet Gherkins Pickles**
5. **Bread and Butter Pickles**
6. **Black Olives**
7. **Marinated Artichokes**

Thanksgiving Rolls with Honey and Nut Butter

1. **2 Containers Refrigerated Rolls or Prepared Rolls**
2. **1/2 Cup Honey**
3. **1 Stick Butter (softened)**
4. **1/4 Cup Finely Chopped Pecans**

If using refrigerated rolls, bake according to container directions. Whip butter at medium speed with mixer until fluffy. Add honey and continue to beat until light and fluffy. Add nuts and mix thoroughly. Refrigerate until ready to serve with rolls.

Pumpkin Pie

1. 1 Can (16 oz.) Pumpkin
2. 1 Can (14 oz.) Sweetened Condensed Milk
3. 2 Eggs (beaten)
4. 1 Teaspoon Pumpkin Pie Spice

Preheat oven to 425 degrees. Combine all the above ingredients and mix well. Pour into unbaked pie shell. Bake 15 minutes at 425 degrees; then reduce heat to 350 degrees and bake an additional 35-40 minutes. **Helpful Hint**: Make pie in advance.

Pecan Pie

Unbaked Pie Shell

1. 3 Eggs (beaten)
2. 1 Cup Sugar
3. 3/4 Cup White Corn Syrup
4. 1 Cup Chopped Pecans

Preheat oven to 325 degrees. Mix all the above ingredients and place into unbaked pie shell. Bake at 325 degrees for 1 hour or until inserted knife comes out clean. **Helpful Hint**: Make pie in advance.

Thanksgiving Shopping List

Produce

___ Fresh Rosemary Sprigs (6-8)
___ 1 Bag (12 oz.) Fresh Cranberries
___ 5 Pounds Potatoes
___ 2 Heads Cauliflower
___ 3 Bananas

Meat

___ 14-15 Pounds Turkey

Pantry Items

___ Flour
___ Sugar
___ 2 Jars (6 oz. each) Sliced Mushrooms
___ 2 Cans (14.5 oz. each) Chicken Broth
___ 1 Package (16 oz.) Pepperidge Farm Herbed Dressing
___ 1 Jar (12 oz.) Orange Marmalade
___ 3 Cups Pecan Pieces
___ 1 Bag (10 oz.) Toasted Coconut Marshmallows
___ 2 Jars (24 oz. each) Mandarin Oranges
___ 2 Jars (24.5 oz each) Pineapple Chunks
___ 1 Cup Sweetened Flaked Coconut
___ 1/2 Cup Honey
___ 1 Can (14 oz.) Sweetened Condensed Milk
___ 3/4 Cup White Corn Syrup
___ 2 Cans (29 oz. each) Sweet Potatoes
___ 1/3 Cup Mayonnaise
___ 1 Can (16 oz.) Pumpkin

Spices

___ 2 Tablespoons Salt Free McCormick All-Purpose Seasoning
___ 2 Tablespoons + 1 teaspoon Pumpkin Pie Spice Mix
___ 2 Teaspoons Vegetable Supreme Seasoning (plus additional for sprinkling)
___ Salt/Pepper

Frozen and Refrigerated Products

___ 3 Sticks Butter
___ 1 Package (4 oz.) Cream Cheese
___ 1 Container (8 oz.) Dill Dip with Real Sour Cream
___ 1 Cup Milk
___ 1 Cup Freshly Grated Parmesan Cheese
___ 2 Containers Refrigerated Rolls
___ 2 (9-inch) Unbaked Pie Shells
___ 5 Eggs

Miscellaneous

___ Add Your Selections For Relish Tray

Christmas Eve Mexican Dinner

Christmas Eve brings a blending of Mexico and Texas to my family's table. Tamales are the centerpiece of our menu. Each year we seek out homemade tamales to be a part of our celebration dinner. Mexican flavors, especially tamales, seem to be traditional with many families – especially in the southwest. If your family enjoys the flavors of Mexican food, perhaps you would enjoy this menu for Christmas Eve or for any other celebration during the year!

Linda Coffee

Christmas Margaritas

Salsa

Sausage Stuffed Jalapenos

Tomato Stuffed Guacamole Salad

Tamale Casserole

Peppered Pinto Beans

Cole Slaw

Mexican Fruit Dish

Praline Cookie Squares

Christmas Margaritas

1. 1 Can (6 oz.) Limeade Concentrate
2. 2/3 Limeade Can Tequila
3. 1/3 Limeade Can Triple Sec
4. 1 Small Carton Frozen Strawberries

Place all of the above ingredients into a blender. Fill the blender with ice and blend until smooth. Pour into margarita glasses.

Salsa

1. 2 Cans (14 1/2 oz.) Diced Tomatoes with Garlic and Onions
2. 2 Serrano Peppers (seeded, membrane removed, and finely diced)
3. 1 Tablespoon Lime Juice
4. 1/8 to 1/4 Cup Fresh Cilantro

In food processor, dice the peppers and cilantro. Add tomatoes and lime juice and pulsate once. The ingredients should be mixed and not soupy. Place into a serving bowl and refrigerate. Serve with corn chips or tortilla chips. **Hint**: Pierce the lime and place into microwave for 10 seconds. This will allow you to get the most juice out of the lime.

Sausage Stuffed Jalapenos

1. **1 Package (16 oz.) Ground Sausage**
2. **1 Package (8 oz.) Cream Cheese (softened)**
3. **1 Cup Grated Cheddar Cheese**
4. **16 Large Jalapeno Peppers (washed, seeded and membranes removed)**

On stovetop, brown the sausage until cooked through. Remove from pan and place on paper towel to drain. Crumble sausage. In mixing bowl, combine cheeses and add crumbled sausage. Mix together thoroughly. Stuff into seeded jalapeno pepper halves. Place stuffed jalapenos on lightly sprayed cookie sheet and bake at 425 degrees for 15-20 minutes.

Tomato Stuffed Guacamole Salad

1. **4 Large Hass Avocados (peeled and seed removed)**
2. **4 Medium Tomatoes (cut in half)**
3. **1/2 Onion (diced)**
4. **3 Tablespoons Fresh Lemon Juice**

In medium bowl, mash the avocados and add the diced onion. Remove the pulp from the tomatoes and dice pulp. Add to the avocadoes and mix. Retain the tomato halves. Pour the lemon juice over the avocado mixture and mix well. Divide the guacamole into eight scoops and place in the reserved tomato shells. Cover with plastic wrap and refrigerate until ready to serve.

Tamale Casserole

1. **3 Pounds Tamales (shucks removed and cut in 2-inch pieces)**
2. **1 Can (10 3/4 oz.) Cream of Chicken Soup**
3. **2 Cans (10 oz. each) Original Rotel Tomatoes and Green Chilies**
4. **2 Cups Monterrey Jack Cheese (grated)**

Preheat oven to 350 degrees. Place cut tamales in lightly greased casserole. Mix soup, Rotel tomatoes and 1 cup of cheese. Pour over tamales and sprinkle remaining cup of cheese over top of casserole. Bake at 350 degrees for 30 minutes or until bubbly.

Peppered Pinto Beans

1. **1 Can (3 lb. 5 oz) Pinto Beans**
2. **2 Slices Peppered Bacon (cut into 1/2-inch strips)**
3. **1 1/2 Cups Beer**
4. **1/2 Cup Mild Picante Sauce**

In large skillet, sauté peppered bacon. Add beer and picante sauce. Reduce heat and simmer 2-3 minutes to reduce some of the fluid. Add beans and continue to simmer for 10 minutes or until beans are thoroughly heated.

Cole Slaw

1. 1 Bag (16 oz.) Cole Slaw Mix
2. 1/2 Onion (finely chopped)
3. 1 Red Pepper (finely chopped)
4. 1 Cup Cole Slaw Dressing

Mix cole slaw mix with onion and pepper. Toss with dressing, place into a serving bowl and refrigerate until ready to serve.

Mexican Fruit Dish

1. 1 Jar (24 1/2 oz.) Pineapple Chunks in Light Syrup (drained)
2. 1 Jar (24 oz.) Mandarin Oranges (drained)
3. 2 Tablespoons Lime Juice
4. 1/8 Teaspoon Chili Powder

In serving bowl, combine pineapple chunks and mandarin oranges. Add lime juice and chili powder and gently toss and mix well. Refrigerate until ready to serve.

Praline Cookie Squares

1   14-15 Cinnamon Graham Cracker Cookies
2. 1 Cup Butter
3. 1 Cup Light Brown Sugar
4. 1 1/2 Cups Chopped Pecans

Preheat oven to 350 degrees. Lightly spray a 15x10x1-inch jellyroll pan. Place enough graham crackers on pan to cover. In saucepan bring butter, brown sugar and pecans to a boil. Boil 2 minutes, stirring constantly. Remove from heat and spread over the tops of the graham crackers. Bake at 350 degrees for 10 minutes. Remove from oven and cool. When cooled, cut into squares.

Christmas Eve Mexican Dinner Shopping List

Produce
- __ 2 Serrano Peppers
- __ 3 Tablespoons Lime Juice
- __ 3 Tablespoons Lemon Juice
- __ Fresh Cilantro
- __ 1 Bag (16 oz.) Cole Slaw Mix
- __ 4 Medium Tomatoes
- __ 1 Onion
- __ 1 Red Pepper
- __ 4 Large Hass Avocados
- __ 16 Large Jalapeno Peppers

Bread, Crackers, Chips
- __ 14-15 Cinnamon Graham Cracker Cookies
- __ Fritos
- __ Tortilla Chips

Meat
- __ 3 Pounds Tamales
- __ 2 Slices Peppered Bacon
- __ 1 Package (16 oz.) Ground Sausage

Pantry Items
- __ 2 Cans (14 1/2 oz. each) Diced Tomato with Garlic and Onions
- __ 1 Can (10 3/4 oz.) Cream of Chicken Soup
- __ 2 Cans (10 oz. each) Original Rotel Tomatoes and Green Chiles
- __ 1 Can (3 lb. 5 oz.) Pinto Beans
- __ 1/2 Cup Mild Picante Sauce
- __ 1 Cup Cole Slaw Dressing
- __ 1 Jar (24 oz.) Pineapple Chunks in Light Syrup
- __ 1 Jar (24 oz.) Mandarin Oranges
- __ 1 Cup Light Brown Sugar
- __ 1 1/2 Cup Chopped Pecans

Spices
- __ 1/8 Teaspoon Chili Powder

Frozen and Refrigerated Products
- __ 2 Cups Grated Monterrey Jack Cheese
- __ 1 Cup Butter
- __ 1 Package (8 oz.) Cream Cheese
- __ 1 Cup Grated Cheddar Cheese

Miscellaneous
- __ 1 1/2 Cups Beer

Christmas Eve Salmon Dinner

After your family and friends have arrived for Christmas, some people like to celebrate Christmas Eve with a more formal type sit-down dinner party. This menu is one of our favorites for making formal seem so easy. You can enjoy this time visiting with everyone too.

Emily Cale

Christmas Martini

Parmesan Caesar Salad

Salmon With Lemon Sauce

Twice Baked Potatoes

Bacon Wrapped Asparagus

Bleu Cheese Rolls

Cherries Jubilee With Ice Cream

Christmas Martini

1. **2 Ounces Skyy Vodka**
2. **3 Ounces Pomegranate Juice**
3. **1 Ounce Cointreau**
4. **Squeeze Of One Lemon**

Place above ingredients into cocktail shaker and add crushed ice. Shake for about 15 seconds and strain into a chilled martini glass. Garnish with a lemon twist. Serves two.

Parmesan Caesar Salad

1. **2 Packages (10 oz. each) Italian Romaine Lettuce**
2. **1/4 Cup Creamy Caesar with Aged Parmesan Salad Dressing**
3. **1/2 Cup Garlic Croutons**
4. **1/3 Cup Fresh Shaved Parmesan Cheese**

In serving bowl, toss together the Romaine lettuce and salad dressing. Top with garlic croutons and shaved Parmesan cheese.

Salmon With Lemon Sauce

1. **2 Packages (16 oz. each) Frozen Salmon Fillets (thawed)**
2. **4 Tablespoons Mayonnaise**
3. **4 Tablespoons Fresh Lemon Juice**
4. **2 Teaspoon Dijon Mustard**

Preheat over to 375 degrees. Place salmon steaks onto a large lightly sprayed baking pan. Spray salmon steaks with cooking spray. Bake at 375 degrees for 8-12 minutes or until fish flakes when pierced with a fork. In a small bowl, mix the mayonnaise, fresh lemon juice and mustard to make the sauce. Refrigerate sauce until ready to serve with salmon.

Twice Baked Potatoes

1. **4 Large Baking Potatoes**
2. **1/2 Cup Sour Cream**
3. **1/2 Cup Milk (warmed)**
4. **4 Tablespoons Butter (melted)**

Preheat oven to 400 degrees. Wash and dry potatoes and lightly grease with vegetable oil or any oil you have in the cupboard. Bake for 1 hour or until tender. Remove from oven and set aside to cool slightly. Half potatoes lengthwise and carefully scoop flesh into a mixing bowl. Reserve skins for filling. Heat oven to 350 degrees. Whip milk, butter, sour cream and season to taste with potato flesh until mixture is smooth. Fill potato skins with mixture and bake at 350 degrees for 20-25 minutes or until heated through. **Suggestion**: Prepare potatoes ahead and refrigerate until ready to be heated prior to serving.

Bacon Wrapped Asparagus

1. **2 Bunches Fresh Asparagus (washed and tough stems removed)**
2. **4 Bacon Slices (cut in half lengthwise)**
3. **1 Jar (12 oz.) Whole Roasted Red Peppers**
4. **1 Lemon**

Preheat oven to 400 degrees. Divide asparagus into eight equal bundles. Remove largest red peppers from jar and slice into eight long slivers. Place one pepper sliver on top of each asparagus bundle. Wrap bacon in a spiral around each bundle and place on a light sprayed baking dish with bacon ends down. Squeeze lemon juice from one lemon evenly over asparagus bundles. Bake at 400 degrees for 30 minutes or until bacon is done and asparagus are tender.

Bleu Cheese Rolls

1. **1/4 Cup Butter**
2. **1/2 Cup Bleu Cheese Crumbles**
3. **2 Ounces Cream Cheese**
4. **2 Packages (11.3 oz each) Refrigerator Dinner Rolls**

Preheat oven to 400 degrees. In a saucepan, over low heat, melt butter, bleu cheese and cream cheese. Whisk together to combine. Cut rolls in half and dip each half into butter/cheese mixture. Place two roll halves into each cup of a standard muffin tin that has been sprayed with cooking spray. Bake at 400 degrees for 10-12 minutes.

Cherries Jubilee With Ice Cream

1. **2 Cans (16 oz. each) Pitted Dark Sweet Cherries**
2. **1/2 Cup Sugar**
3. **1/4 Cup Cornstarch**
4. **1/2 Cup Brandy**

Drain cherries, reserving syrup. On stovetop in saucepan, blend sugar and cornstarch. Gradually stir in reserved syrup, mixing well. Cook and stir over medium heat until mixture is thickened and bubbly. Remove from heat, stir in cherries. Turn mixture into a chafing dish or blazer pan. Place chafing dish at the dinner table along with individual bowls of ice cream for your guests. Heat brandy in small saucepan. Pour heated brandy into a large ladle. At the table, ignite the brandy so it flames. While it is flaming, pour onto the cherries jubilee. Stir to blend brandy into the sauce. **Note**: Brandy will continue to flame for awhile, even while you serve the cherries jubilee over the ice cream.

Christmas Eve Salmon Dinner Shopping List

Produce

__ 2 Packages (10 oz. each) Italian Romaine
   Lettuce
__ 3 Lemons
__ 4 Large Baking Potatoes
__ 2 Bunches Fresh Asparagus

Bread, Crackers, Chips

__ 1/2 Cup Garlic Croutons

Meat

__ 2 Packages (16 oz. each) Frozen Salmon
   Fillets
__ 4 Slices Bacon

Pantry Items

__ 1/4 Cup Creamy Caesar with Aged
   Parmesan Salad Dressing
__ 4 Tablespoons Mayonnaise
__ 2 Teaspoons Dijon Mustard
__ 1 Jar (12 oz.) Whole Roasted Red Peppers
__ 1/2 Cup Sugar
__ 1/4 Cup Cornstarch
__ 2 Cans (16 oz. each) Pitted Dark Sweet
   Cherries

Frozen and Refrigerated Products

__ 1/3 Cup Shaved Parmesan Cheese
__ 1/2 Cup Sour Cream
__ 1/2 Cup Milk
__ 1/2 Cup Butter
__ 1/2 Cup Bleu Cheese Crumbles
__ 2 Ounces Cream Cheese
__ 2 Packages (11.3 oz. each) Refrigerator
   Dinner Rolls
__ 1 Gallon Homemade Vanilla Ice Cream

Miscellaneous

__ 1/2 Cup Brandy

Christmas Day

Christmas is celebrated all over the world and in many different ways. In our families this is the holiday we unite with our loved ones. These special recipes are prepared with lots of love. Merry Christmas!

Linda and Emily

Christmas Fruit Salad

Garlic Peppered Standing Rib Roast

Parsley New Potatoes and Pearl Onions

Hazelnut Brussels Sprouts

Almond Green Beans

Wreath of Rolls

Eggnog Panettoni Bread Pudding with Sauce

Christmas Fruit Salad

1. 1 Package (12 oz.) Fresh Cranberries
2. 3 Medium Apples (cored)
3. 1 Cup Sugar
4. 2 Cups Cool Whip

In food processor, chop cranberries and apples until fine. Add sugar and pulse several times to combine. Remove to bowl and gently fold in Cool Whip. Spread mixture into casserole dish. Cover tightly and place in freezer overnight. Prior to serving, remove from freezer, defrost slightly and cut into squares.
Serving Idea: Serve on a dark green bed of lettuce.

Garlic Peppered Standing Rib Roast

1. 7 Pounds Standing Rib Roast Bone-In
2. 2 Tablespoons Course Black Pepper
3. 1 Teaspoon Lowry's Seasoned Salt
4. 1 Teaspoon Garlic Powder

Preheat oven to 450 degrees. Mix pepper, salt and garlic powder and rub on the standing rib roast. Place roast on a rack in a roasting pan. Bake uncovered at 450 degrees for 10 minutes. Reduce heat to 300 degrees and continue to bake uncovered for 2 to 2 1/2 hours. For a medium cooked roast, meat thermometer should reach 135 degrees when placed into center of roast. Remove roast from oven and cover with foil for 15 minutes before slicing.

Parsley New Potatoes and Pearl Onions

1. **2 Pounds Red New Potatoes**
2. **1 Pound White Pearl Onions**
3. **3 Tablespoons Extra Virgin Olive Oil**
4. **2 Tablespoons Fresh Rosemary (chopped)**

Preheat oven to 400 degrees. Wash and peel around center only of the new potatoes. Place into a lightly sprayed large casserole dish. Cut tips off pearl onion and peel away the outer skin of the onions and place into casserole with the potatoes. In small mixing bowl, combine olive oil and rosemary. Pour over potatoes and onions and mix until they are coated. Cover casserole and place into oven and bake at 400 degrees for 20 minutes. Turn potatoes and onions and continue baking an additional 20 minutes. Season to taste.

Hazelnut Brussels Sprouts

1. **2 Pounds Fresh Brussels Sprouts**
2. **1/4 Cup Maple Syrup**
3. **1/4 Cup Butter (melted)**
4. **1/4 Cup Hazelnuts (chopped)**

Wash Brussels sprouts and remove outer layer. Cut larger sprouts in half. Bring 8 cups of water to a boil and add the Brussels sprouts. Return to a boil and cook approximately 10 minutes or until sprouts are tender, but not mushy. Drain sprouts and place into an 8x8-inch casserole dish. In mixing bowl, combine maple syrup, butter and hazelnuts. Pour over sprouts and toss gently until coated. Serve warm.

Almond Green Beans

1. **1 1/2 Pounds (6 cups) Fresh Green Beans (cut into 1-inch pieces)**
2. **1 Tablespoon Lemon Juice**
3. **2 Tablespoons Butter (melted)**
4. **1/4 Cup Sliced Almonds**

Toast almonds in a small skillet sprayed with cooking spray over medium heat until golden, about 5-7 minutes, stirring constantly so they won't burn. Remove from pan and set aside. Cook fresh green beans in a covered saucepan in a small amount of boiling water for 12-15 minutes or until crisp-tender. Drain. Mix together lemon juice and melted butter in a small bowl. Pour over green beans and toss to coat. Gently stir in toasted almonds. **Suggestion**: Almonds can be toasted up to 2 days ahead and stored in an airtight container.

Wreath of Rolls

1. **2 Cans (16.3 oz each) Jumbo Flaky Style Biscuits**
2. **1/2 Cup Butter (melted)**
3. **1 Tablespoon Finely Chopped Onion**
4. **2 Tablespoons Finely Chopped Fresh Chives**

Preheat oven to 350 degrees. In a bowl, combine the butter and onion. Open the can of biscuits and cut each biscuit in half. Brush each biscuit half in the butter mixture. On a lightly sprayed pizza pan, stand biscuits on their cut edge. With biscuits touching, arrange in a wreath type circle. Sprinkle with chives and bake at 350 degrees for 18-20 minutes or until biscuits are golden brown in color.

Eggnog Panettoni Bread Pudding With Sauce

1. **5 Cups Panettoni Bread (cut into very small pieces)**
2. **1/2 Cup Pecan Pieces or Walnut Pieces**
3. **3 Cups plus 1 Cup (for sauce) Prepared Eggnog**
4. **1/3 Cup plus 2 Teaspoons (for sauce) Bourbon**

Preheat oven to 475 degrees. On stovetop, heat a pot of water (approximately 2 cups) for use later. In a large mixing bowl, combine panettoni bread pieces, nut pieces, 3 cups eggnog and 1/3 cup bourbon. Spray a 12 hole muffin tin with cooking spray and ladle bread/eggnog mixture evenly into the muffin tins. Top surface will not be smooth. Place muffin tin onto a baking sheet with sides. Place into preheated oven and pour the heated water into the baking sheet around the muffin tin. This creates a water bath around the muffin tin. Bake at 475 degrees for 15-20 minutes until the tops are nicely browned and a toothpick comes clean from the center. Remove muffin tin from oven. **Safety warning**: Leave water in oven on the baking sheet to cool. Let the bread pudding cool slightly before removing from the tins. **Suggestion**: Bread pudding can be made earlier in the day.

Sauce for Bread Pudding: On stovetop combine the remaining 1 cup eggnog and 2 teaspoons bourbon in a saucepan and heat until warm, but not boiling. Serve hot on top of bread pudding.

Christmas Day Shopping List

Produce
___ 2 Pounds Red New Potatoes
___ 1 Pound White Pearl Onions
___ 2 Tablespoons Fresh Rosemary
___ 2 Pounds Fresh Brussels Sprouts
___ 1 1/2 Pounds Fresh Green Beans
___ 1 Lemon (1 tablespoon lemon juice)
___ 1 Package (12 oz.) Fresh Cranberries
___ 3 Medium Apples
___ 1 Tablespoon Chopped Onion
___ 2 Tablespoons Finely Chopped Chives

Bread, Crackers, Chips
___ 5 Cups Panettoni Bread

Meat
___ 7 Pounds Standing Rib Roast Bone-In

Pantry Items
___ 3 Tablespoons Extra Virgin Olive Oil
___ 1/4 Cup Maple Syrup
___ 1/4 Cup Chopped Hazelnuts
___ 1/4 Cup Sliced Almonds
___ 1 Cup Sugar
___ 1/2 Cup Pecan Pieces

Spices
___ 2 Tablespoons Coarse Black Pepper
___ 1 Teaspoon Lowry's Seasoned Salt
___ 1 Teaspoon Garlic Powder

Frozen and Refrigerated Products
___ 2 Sticks Butter
___ 2 Cups Cool Whip
___ 1 Quart Eggnog
___ 2 Cans (16.3 oz.) Jumbo Flaky Style
     Biscuits

Miscellaneous
___ Bourbon

Recipes by

Categories

Drinks and Beverages

Bubbles and Beads

We suggest you start this party with an easy Champagne drink. Have your champagne glasses ready for your guests when they arrive by placing a few dried cranberries in each Champagne glass. When your guests arrive, pour the Champagne over the cranberries and serve immediately. The cranberries will float around the glass.

Christmas Margaritas

1. **1 Can (6 oz.) Limeade Concentrate**
2. **2/3 Limeade Can Tequila**
3. **1/3 Limeade Can Triple Sec**
4. **1 Small Carton Frozen Strawberries**

Place all of the above ingredients into a blender. Fill the blender with ice and blend until smooth. Pour into margarita glasses.

Christmas Martini

1. **2 Ounces Skyy Vodka**
2. **3 Ounces Pomegranate Juice**
3. **1 Ounce Cointreau**
4. **Squeeze Of One Lemon**

Place above ingredients into cocktail shaker and add crushed ice. Shake for about 15 seconds and strain into a chilled martini glass. Garnish with a lemon twist. Serves two.

Individual Chocolate Peppermint Coffee (1 Cup of Coffee)

1. **1 Ounce Kahlua**
2. **2/3 Cup Hot Black Coffee**
3. **Sweetener To Taste**
4. **Peppermint Whipping Cream (by Land O Lake)**

Pour Kahlua into a cup of hot coffee. Add sweetener to the coffee if you like. Top with a squirt of peppermint whipping cream. **Serving Idea**: Use a peppermint stick for a stir.

Ladies Mimosa With Strawberries

1. 1 Bottle of Champagne (chilled)
2. 1 Carton of Orange Juice
3. Fresh Strawberries (sliced)
4. Sugar

For each serving, fill half of the champagne glass with chilled champagne. Fill the remainder of the glass with orange juice and gently stir. Dip each strawberry slice in sugar. Place strawberry slice on the rim of each glass.

Southern Mint Tea

1. 2 Cups Water Plus Additional Water to Make 1 Gallon Tea
2. 2 Bags Plantation Mint Tea
3. 2 Family Size Bags of Regular Tea
4. 2/3 Cup Sugar

In microwave, heat 2 cups water for about 5 minutes on high. Remove from microwave and add the mint tea and regular tea bags. Allow to steep for 10 minutes. Place 3 quarts of cold water in a one-gallon pitcher. Add sugar and concentrated tea to the pitcher. Stir. Add additional water to completely fill pitcher. Cover and refrigerate until ready to serve. **Serving Idea**: Garnish with fresh mint leaves.

Artichoke Pesto Gratin

1. **2 Cans (10 oz. each) Artichoke Hearts (drained)**
2. **1/4 Cup Sundried Tomato Pesto**
3. **1 Cup Shredded Romano Cheese (3/4 cup in mix and 1/4 cup for top)**
4. **1/2 Cup Mayonnaise**

Preheat oven to 350 degrees. In food processor or blender, chop artichokes. Add pesto, 3/4 cup Romano cheese and mayonnaise. Blend for 5 seconds. Place into a lightly sprayed 9x13-inch glass-baking dish. Sprinkle remaining 1/4 cup cheese over top and bake at 350 degrees for 20-25 minutes or until bubbly. Serve hot with garlic panetini bread.

Beef Stick Stacks

1. 1 Pound Beef Stick Summer Sausage
2. 1 Jar (15 oz.) Whole Pearl Onions
3. 1 Container (8 oz.) Fresh Mozzarella Cheese Balls
4. 1 Jar (14 oz.) Mild Peppedews (whole sweet piquante peppers)

Unwrap and slice the beef stick into 1/4-inch slices. Stuff one peppedew with one cheese ball. If cheese balls are too large, cut in half. Place on top of slice of beef stick and top with one onion. Stick a toothpick down through center of onion and peppedew into sausage. Place on a large platter, cover and refrigerate until ready to serve.

Black Bean, Roasted Red Pepper Pate

1. 1 Can (15 oz.) Black Beans (rinsed and drained)
2. 1/2 Cup Roasted Red Peppers
3. 1 Package (8 oz.) Cream Cheese (softened)
4. 1 Tablespoon Regina Champagne Wine Vinegar

In food processor, combine above ingredients and blend until smooth in texture. Place in a serving bowl, cover and refrigerate until ready to serve. Serve with Melba toast rounds or assorted crackers.

Chicken Chili Pom Poms

1. **1 1/4 Pounds Boneless, Skinless Chicken Breasts (about 4 breasts)**
2. **12 Slices Bacon**
3. **2/3 Cup Firmly Packed Brown Sugar**
4. **1 Tablespoon Chili Powder**

Preheat oven to 375 degrees. Cut chicken breasts into 1-inch cubes. Cut bacon slice into thirds. Wrap each chicken cube with a piece of bacon and secure with a toothpick. Stir together brown sugar and chili powder. Dredge wrapped chicken in brown sugar mixture. Coat a rack and broiler pan with nonstick cooking spray. Place wrapped chicken on rack and bake at 375 degrees for 30-35 minutes or until bacon is crisp and chicken is done.

Deviled Eggs

1. **1 Dozen Eggs (hard boiled)**
2. **1/4 Cup Dill Pickle Relish**
3. **1/3 Cup Mayonnaise**
4. **2 Teaspoons Mustard**

Shell eggs, cut in half lengthwise, and remove yolks. In small mixing bowl, mash yolks, and mix dill pickle relish, mayonnaise and mustard. Fill centers of whites with yolk mixture. Cover and refrigerate until ready to serve. Makes 24 deviled eggs. **Helpful Hint**: The fresher the egg, the more difficult it is to peel.

First Down Veggie Dip

1. 1 Cup Sour Cream
2. 1/4 Cup Chicken Wing Sauce
3. 1/2 Cup Finely Chopped Celery
4. Assorted Fresh Vegetables

In serving bowl, mix the first three ingredients and refrigerate until ready to serve. Wash and cut the assorted vegetables to serve with the dip.

Hot Cheese Punts

1. 1 Package (8 oz.) Grated Sharp Cheddar Cheese
2. 1 Pound Ground Hot Sausage
3. 3 1/2 Cups Biscuit Mix
4. 1 Can (4.5 oz.) Diced Green Chiles

Preheat oven to 375 degrees. Mix above ingredients and roll into 1-inch balls. Place on lightly sprayed baking sheet. Bake at 375 degrees for 10-15 minutes.
Helpful Hint: These can be made ahead and frozen on a cookie sheet and then stored in a plastic bag until ready to thaw and bake.

Olive Cheese Ball Pumpkin Appetizers

1. **16-18 Medium Pimento Stuffed Green Olives (drained and dried)**
2. **1/2 Cup Flour**
3. **1/4 Cup Butter (melted)**
4. **1 Cup Finely Grated Extra Sharp Cheddar Cheese**

Preheat oven to 400 degrees. In a small bowl, combine and mix well the flour, butter and cheddar cheese to form a smooth dough. Wrap a small amount of this mixture around each olive, about 1 teaspoon or enough to cover the olive. Place on a lightly sprayed cookie sheet and bake at 400 degrees for 12 minutes. **Suggestion**: You can make these olives ahead of time and refrigerate until you are ready to bake them.

Olive Martini Appetizers

1. **1 Jar (10 oz.) Jalapeno Stuffed Olives**
2. **1 Jar (10 oz.) Garlic Stuffed Olives**
3. **1 Jar (10 oz.) Calamari Olives**
4. **1 Jar (10 oz.) Anchovy Stuffed Olives**

Drain and place each of the different types of olives into four individual martini glasses. Serve with festive holiday toothpicks. **Serving Idea**: Place the four olive martini appetizers on a decorative silver tray.

Party Field Goals

1. **2 Pounds Frozen Cooked Meatballs**
2. **1 Tablespoon Prepared Mustard**
3. **1 Bottle (12 oz.) Chili Sauce**
4. **1 Jar (10 oz.) Jalapeno Jelly**

On stovetop or crock-pot, mix together chili sauce, jalapeno jelly and mustard. Carefully stir in meatballs. Simmer, stirring occasionally, 30-40 minutes or until meatballs are thoroughly heated. Keep warm in crock-pot or stovetop.

"Philly" Steak Squares

1. **1 Package (16 oz.) Philly Beef Steak with Onions and Green Peppers**
2. **1 Can (6 oz.) Portabella Mushroom Steak Sauce**
3. **1 Package (8 oz.) Four Cheese Pizza Cheese**
4. **1 Can (13.8 oz.) Refrigerated Pizza Crust**

Preheat oven to 375 degrees. On stovetop, in large frying pan, cook Philly beef steak according to package directions, adding 1/2 of the mushroom sauce to the meat while it is cooking. Set aside. On a lightly sprayed 9x13-inch baking sheet, unroll the pizza crust and pat dough until it fills most of the cookie sheet. Spread the rest of the mushroom sauce over the top of the pizza crust. Spread the Philly steak mixture over the mushroom sauce and top with cheese. Bake at 375 degrees for 20 minutes. Remove from oven and cool slightly. Slice the pizza into squares. Serve warm.

Pineapple Coconut Fruit Dip

1. **1 Can (8 oz.) Crushed Pineapple (undrained)**
2. **1 Package (3 1/2 oz.) Instant Coconut Pudding Mix**
3. **3/4 Cup Milk**
4. **1/2 Cup Sour Cream**

In food processor, add crushed pineapple, coconut pudding mix, milk and sour cream. Process for at least 30 seconds. Pour into serving bowl and refrigerate for 2 hours or overnight. This will allow flavors to blend. Serve with assortment of fresh fruit. Serving Idea: Slice a fresh pineapple in half lengthwise and hollow out inside of pineapple to use as a fresh fruit bowl. Place some of the fresh pineapple around the dip along with the other fruit.

Red and White Pinwheels

1. **Spinach or Tomato Flour Tortillas (we used three 10-inch tortillas)**
2. **1 Package (8 oz.) Cream Cheese (soften)**
3. **1/2 to 1 Can (4 oz.) Chopped Green Chiles (drained)**
4 **1 Jar (4 oz.) Chopped Red Pimentos (drained)**

Beat cream cheese until smooth. Add green chiles and red pimentos and mix to combine. Spread mixture on surface of each tortilla to the edge. Roll tortilla tightly and place in airtight container and refrigerate at least two hours. Slice each roll into 1-inch slices forming a pinwheel. Arrange on platter to serve.

Salsa

1. 2 Cans (14 1/2 oz.) Diced Tomatoes with Garlic and Onions
2. 2 Serrano Peppers (seeded, membrane removed, and finely diced)
3. 1 Tablespoon Lime Juice
4. 1/8 to 1/4 Cup Fresh Cilantro

In food processor, dice the peppers and cilantro. Add tomatoes and lime juice and pulsate once. The ingredients should be mixed and not soupy. Place into a serving bowl and refrigerate. Serve with corn chips or tortilla chips. **Hint**: Pierce the lime and place into microwave for 10 seconds. This will allow you to get the most juice out of the lime.

Sausage Stuffed Jalapenos

1. 1 Package (16 oz.) Ground Sausage
2. 1 Package (8 oz.) Cream Cheese (softened)
3. 1 Cup Grated Cheddar Cheese
4. 16 Large Jalapeno Peppers (washed, seeded and membranes removed)

On stovetop, brown the sausage until cooked through. Remove from pan and place on paper towel to drain. Crumble sausage. In mixing bowl, combine cheeses and add crumbled sausage. Mix together thoroughly. Stuff into seeded jalapeno pepper halves. Place stuffed jalapenos on lightly sprayed cookie sheet and bake at 425 degrees for 15-20 minutes.

Shrimp Skewer Sparklers

1. **2 Pounds Medium Fresh Cooked Shrimp**
2. **1 Fresh Pineapple (cut into chunks)**
3. **1 Bag (12 oz.) Cherry Tomatoes**
4. **1 Bottle Sesame Ginger Salad Dressing (Paul Newman)**

If using wooden skewers, remember to soak in water before putting the food on them. This will prevent them from burning when you broil. Alternate and arrange shrimp, pineapple chunks, and cherry tomatoes on skewers. Place in casserole dish and pour salad dressing over the skewers to marinate. Cover with plastic wrap and refrigerate until ready to broil. Remove from refrigerator, place on baking sheet and brush with dressing from the casserole dish. Broil approximately 2 minutes per side - remember the shrimp is already cooked. **Suggestion**: These shrimp skewers are also good grilled.

Smoked Salmon Log

1. **1 Package (8 oz.) Cream Cheese (softened)**
2. **1 Package (4 oz.) Smoked Salmon (flaked)**
3. **2 Tablespoons Green Onions (finely chopped)**
4. **2 Tablespoons Celery (finely chopped)**

Combine above ingredients and shape into a log. Refrigerate until ready to serve. Serve with assorted crackers.

Stuffed Mushrooms

1. 1 Pound Fresh Whole Mushrooms (half dollar size)
2. 1 Cup Bread (cubed into very small pieces)
3. 3 Tablespoons Butter (melted)
4. 2 Slices Sandwich Ham (chopped into small pieces)

Preheat oven to 350 degrees. Clean and remove stems from mushrooms. Chop stems and place into a bowl. Add cut up bread, melted butter and chopped ham. Mix well and stuff into mushroom caps. Place mushrooms onto a lightly sprayed casserole dish and bake at 350 degrees for 15 minutes.

Summer Salsa

1. 1 Can (28 oz.) Bush's Original Baked Beans
2. 1 Can (14.5 oz.) Diced Tomatoes With Jalapenos (drained)
3. 1 Cup Frozen Corn Kernels
4. 1 Cup Chopped Onion

Mix above ingredients in serving bowl. Chill in refrigerator. Serve with tortilla chips, Frito scoops, or sliced fresh baguette bread. **Suggestion**: Can be made a day ahead.

Tasty Cheese Football

1. 1 Package (8 oz.) Cream Cheese (softened)
2. 1 Package (4 oz.) Pastrami (finely chopped)
3. 3 Tablespoons Green Onions (finely chopped)
4. 1/2 Cup Crushed Pecans

Mix cream cheese, pastrami and green onions. Shape into a football. Roll football in crushed pecans until it covers the mixture and looks like a brown football. Serve with assorted crackers.

Touchdown Mix

1. 1 Package (9 3/4 oz.) Flamin' Hot Corn Chips
2. 1 Package (4 oz.) White Cheddar Popcorn
3. 4 Cups Mini Pretzels
4. 2 Cups Dry Roasted Peanuts

In a large serving bowl, mix above ingredients. **Serving Idea**: Serve in individual paper bags.

Soups and Salads

Ambrosia Fruit Salad

1. **2 Jars (24 oz. each) Mandarin Oranges (drained, retain 1/4 cup liquid)**
2. **2 Jars (24.5 oz. each) Pineapple Chunks (drained)**
3. **1 Cup Sweetened Flaked Coconut**
4. **3 Bananas (sliced)**

In serving bowl, add drained mandarin oranges, 1/4 cup of mandarin orange liquid, pineapple chunks, coconut and sliced bananas. Toss. Refrigerate until ready to serve. Serve with a slotted spoon.

Avocado Grapefruit Salad

1. **2 Jars (24 oz. each) Grapefruit Sections (well drained)**
2. **3 Medium Avocados (peeled and chopped)**
3. **1/2 Medium Red Onion (sliced thin)**
4. **1/3 Cup Coleslaw Dressing**

Cut grapefruit sections in bite-sized chunks. Cut thin slices of red onion into 1/2-inch lengths. In salad bowl, combine drained grapefruit sections, avocados and onions. Add coleslaw dressing and gentle toss. Cover and refrigerate until ready to serve. **Suggestion**: Serve on a bed of lettuce.

Black-eyed Pea Salad

1. 2 Cans (15.8 oz. each) Black-eyed Peas (drained and rinsed)
2. 1 Medium Red Bell Pepper (cored and chopped)
3. 1/2 Medium White Onion (chopped)
4. 1/4 Cup Vinaigrette Salad Dressing

In serving bowl, mix above ingredients and chill at least one hour or overnight in refrigerator. Season to taste. Toss before serving. Serve cold.

Bleu Cheese Walnut Salad

1. 2 Bags (5 oz. each) Spring Mix Salad Greens
2. 2/3 Cup Walnut Halves
3. 1/4 Cup Bleu Cheese Crumbles
4. 1/4 Cup Raspberry Walnut Vinaigrette Salad Dressing

Combine salad greens, walnut halves, and bleu cheese crumbles in salad bowl. Cover and refrigerate. Before serving the salad, toss with the Raspberry Walnut Vinaigrette Salad Dressing.

Broccoli Cheese Herb Soup

1. 1 Package (24 oz.) Green Giant Broccoli & Three Cheese Sauce
2. 1 Jar (5 oz.) Old English Sharp Cheese Spread
3. 2 Cans (10 3/4 oz. each) Cream of Chicken with Herbs Soup (plus 2 soup cans of water)
4. 2 Cups Butter Flavored Croutons

Remove cheese sauce chips from the package of broccoli and place in large saucepan. Add Old English Cheese to saucepan with sauce chips and heat over low heat to melt, stirring occasionally. Leave the broccoli in package, allowing it to partially thaw for about 15 minutes. Place broccoli in food processor and process until broccoli is in very small chunks. When cheese is melted, add the two cans of soup and 2 cans of water and stir until well combined. Add the chopped broccoli and continue to heat until warm. Place soup in serving bowls and sprinkle with butter flavored croutons.

Cabbage and Bacon Salad

1. 1 Small Head Cabbage (chopped into small pieces)
2. 1 1/2 Cups Sharp Cheddar Cheese (cut into small cubes)
3. 10 Slices Bacon (cooked and crumbled)
4. 3/4 Cup Roasted Garlic Rice Vinegar

In serving bowl, mix above ingredients and chill at least one hour or overnight in refrigerator. Season to taste. Toss before serving. Serve cold.

Carrot Salad

1. **2 Pounds Whole Carrots (washed, peeled, grated)**
2. **1 Can (8 oz.) Pineapple Tidbits (drained and cut in half)**
3. **1/2 Cup Chopped Pecans**
4. **2/3 Cup Mayonnaise With Lime Juice**

Combine grated carrots, pineapple tidbits and pecans. Toss with mayo dressing. Cover and refrigerate until ready to serve.

Chicken Salad

1. **3 1/2 Cups Cooked Diced Chicken**
2. **2/3 Cup Sweetened Dried Cranberries (chopped)**
3. **2/3 Cup Mayonnaise**
4. **1/2 Cup Almonds (sliced)**

Place diced chicken in mixing bowl. Add mayonnaise and cranberries and stir until well combined. Add almond slices and stir. Cover mixture and refrigerate until ready to serve. **Suggestion**: Place in a mound on plate and garnish with cantaloupe slice.

Chilled Buffalo Bleu Cheese Salad

1. **2 Heads of Iceberg Lettuce (each cut into quarters)**
2. **2 Large Tomatoes (diced)**
3. **1 Bottle Buffalo Bleu Cheese Salad Dressing**
4. **1 Container (8 oz.) Bleu Cheese Crumbles**

Immediately before serving, place the eight quartered lettuce wedges in freezer for about 1-2 minutes to chill. Important: Do not leave lettuce longer or it will freeze. Remove from freezer and sprinkle each wedge with diced tomatoes. Drizzle with Buffalo Bleu Cheese Salad Dressing and sprinkle with Bleu Cheese crumbles.

Chilled Tomato and Cucumber Salad

1. **1 1/2 Pints Small Cherry Tomatoes (cut in half)**
2. **1 Large Burpless Cucumber (peeled)**
3. **1/2 Cup Bottled Ranch Salad Dressing**
4. **1 Tablespoon Rice Vinegar**

Cut peeled cucumber in half lengthwise and then slice into thin slices. In serving bowl, combine tomatoes and cucumbers. In separate bowl, mix ranch dressing with rice vinegar. Pour over tomatoes and cucumbers. Season to taste. Chill until ready to serve.

Christmas Fruit Salad

1. 1 Package (12 oz.) Fresh Cranberries
2. 3 Medium Apples (cored)
3. 1 Cup Sugar
4. 2 Cups Cool Whip

In food processor, chop cranberries and apples until fine. Add sugar and pulse several times to combine. Remove to bowl and gently fold in Cool Whip. Spread mixture into casserole dish. Cover tightly and place in freezer overnight. Prior to serving, remove from freezer, defrost slightly and cut into squares.
Serving Idea: Serve on a dark green bed of lettuce.

Cole Slaw

1. 1 Bag (16 oz.) Cole Slaw Mix
2. 1/2 Onion (finely chopped)
3. 1 Red Pepper (finely chopped)
4. 1 Cup Cole Slaw Dressing

Mix cole slaw mix with onion and pepper. Toss with dressing, place into a serving bowl and refrigerate until ready to serve.

Colorful Spinach Salad

1. **1 Pound Fresh Spinach (washed and dried)**
2. **1/2 Small Head Purple Cabbage**
3. **1 Package (7 oz.) Dried Tropical Fruit Mix**
4. **1 Package (2 oz.) Pecan Pieces**

In serving bowl, tear the spinach and cabbage into bite-sized pieces. Add the fruit mix and pecan pieces. Toss. Serve with a Spinach Vinaigrette Salad Dressing.

Crab Bisque

1. **1 Jar (26 oz.) Tomato Basil Sauce**
2. **2 Cups Half and Half**
3. **1/3 Cup Cooking Sherry or white cooking wine**
4. **1 Can (6 oz.) White Crab Meat (drained)**

Puree tomato sauce in blender or food processor. Place in saucepan and add half and half. Heat on low. Measure 1/3 cup cooking sherry in bowl and add crabmeat. Let marinate for about 15 minutes. Immediately before serving, add crab/sherry mixture to soup and bring to a simmer. Serve hot. **Suggestion**: Sprinkle with flavored toasted bread crumbs or croutons.

Mango and Kiwi Salad

1. 1 Jar (24.5 oz.) Pineapple Chunks (drained)
2. 2 Fresh Mangos (peeled and cubed)
3. 3 Fresh Kiwi Fruit (peeled and sliced)
4. 3 Tablespoons Raspberry Pecan Salad Dressing

In serving bowl, combine and mix pineapple, mango and kiwi slices. Add Raspberry Pecan Salad Dressing. Chill until ready to serve.

Melon Explosion

1. 1 Small Seedless Watermelon
2. 1 Cantaloupe
3. 1 Honey Dew Melon
4. 10 Limes (makes 2/3 cup fresh lime juice)

Using a melon ball scoop, make balls with the insides of the watermelon, cantaloupe and honey dew. Place in bowl. Squeeze eight limes to make fresh lime juice, remove any seeds. Pour lime juice over melon balls and gently toss. Cover and refrigerate until chilled. When ready to serve, remove from the refrigerator, and use a slotted spoon to place melon balls into serving dish. Prior to serving, pour the juice from the remaining two limes over the melon balls. **Serving Idea**: Watermelon cavity can be used as a bowl.

Mexican Fruit Dish

1. 1 Jar (24 1/2 oz.) Pineapple Chunks in Light Syrup (drained)
2. 1 Jar (24 oz.) Mandarin Oranges (drained)
3. 2 Tablespoons Lime Juice
4. 1/8 Teaspoon Chili Powder

In serving bowl, combine pineapple chunks and mandarin oranges. Add lime juice and chili powder and gently toss and mix well. Refrigerate until ready to serve.

Parmesan Caesar Salad

1. 2 Packages (10 oz. each) Italian Romaine Lettuce
2. 1/4 Cup Creamy Caesar with Aged Parmesan Salad Dressing
3. 1/2 Cup Garlic Croutons
4. 1/3 Cup Fresh Shaved Parmesan Cheese

In serving bowl, toss together the Romaine lettuce and salad dressing. Top with garlic croutons and shaved Parmesan cheese.

Potato Salad

1. **3 Pounds Red New Potatoes**
2. **1/3 Cup Cider Vinegar**
3. **2/3 Cup Mayonnaise**
4. **2/3 Cup Green Onions (sliced)**

In saucepan, cover potatoes with water and bring to a boil. Once potatoes boil, cover and reduce heat to medium low, simmering for 10 to15 minutes. Potatoes should be fork tender. Drain and cool slightly. Cut potatoes into quarters or smaller; and while still warm, stir in vinegar. Marinate in vinegar for 30 minutes, stirring occasionally. Drain excess vinegar off and add mayonnaise and green onions. Refrigerate. **Suggestion**: Can be made a day ahead.

Shrimp Salad

1. **1 Pound Medium Fresh Cooked Shrimp**
2. **1/2 Green Pepper (finely chopped)**
3. **2 Green Onions (finely chopped)**
4. **1/4 Cup Lime and Garlic Salsa**

Combine above ingredients, stir and marinate overnight. **Suggestion**: Place on a bed of lettuce or serve with a large slice of avocado.

Spinach and Dried Cranberry Salad

1. **2 Bags (6 oz. each) Baby Spinach (torn into bite-size pieces)**
2. **1/2 Medium Red Onion (sliced)**
3. **1 Package (6 oz.) Dried Sweetened Cranberries**
4. **1/2 Cup Feta Cheese**

In salad bowl, combine above ingredients and toss. Use with Raspberry Vinaigrette Dressing or your favorite vinaigrette salad dressing.

Spring Mix Salad

1. **2 Bags (5 oz. each) Spring Mix Salad Greens**
2. **1 Large Hass Avocado (peeled, halved and sliced)**
3. **1 Bag (12 oz.) Cherry Tomatoes (halved)**
4. **1 Can (6 oz.) Small Pitted Black Olives (drained)**

In serving bowl, combine above ingredients. Cover and refrigerate until ready to serve. Serve or toss with your favorite salad dressing. **Helpful Hint**: Slice avocado in half and twist each half apart; remove seed. Using a large tablespoon, gently scoop avocado half out of peel.

Tomato Stuffed Guacamole Salad

1. **4 Large Hass Avocados (peeled and seed removed)**
2. **4 Medium Tomatoes (cut in half)**
3. **1/2 Onion (diced)**
4. **3 Tablespoons Fresh Lemon Juice**

In medium bowl, mash the avocados and add the diced onion. Remove the pulp from the tomatoes and dice pulp. Add to the avocadoes and mix. Retain the tomato halves. Pour the lemon juice over the avocado mixture and mix well. Divide the guacamole into eight scoops and place in the reserved tomato shells. Cover with plastic wrap and refrigerate until ready to serve.

Tropical Fruit Salad

1. **2 Jars (24 oz. each) Del Monte Tropical Fruit (drained)**
2. **1 Cup Green Grapes**
3. **1/2 Cup Walnut Pieces**
4. **2 Tablespoons Creamy Poppy Seed Salad Dressing**

In serving bowl, mix above ingredients and chill at least one hour. Gently toss before serving. Serve cold.

Almond Green Beans

1. 1 1/2 Pounds (6 cups) Fresh Green Beans (cut into 1-inch pieces)
2. 1 Tablespoon Lemon Juice
3. 2 Tablespoons Butter (melted)
4. 1/4 Cup Sliced Almonds

Toast almonds in a small skillet sprayed with cooking spray over medium heat until golden, about 5-7 minutes, stirring constantly so they won't burn. Remove from pan and set aside. Cook fresh green beans in a covered saucepan in a small amount of boiling water for 12-15 minutes or until crisp-tender. Drain. Mix together lemon juice and melted butter in a small bowl. Pour over green beans and toss to coat. Gently stir in toasted almonds. **Suggestion**: Almonds can be toasted up to 2 days ahead and stored in an airtight container.

Bacon Wrapped Asparagus

1. 2 Bunches Fresh Asparagus (washed and tough stems removed)
2. 4 Bacon Slices (cut in half lengthwise)
3. 1 Jar (12 oz.) Whole Roasted Red Peppers
4. 1 Lemon

Preheat oven to 400 degrees. Divide asparagus into eight equal bundles. Remove largest red peppers from jar and slice into eight long slivers. Place one pepper sliver on top of each asparagus bundle. Wrap bacon in a spiral around each bundle and place on a light sprayed baking dish with bacon ends down. Squeeze lemon juice from one lemon evenly over asparagus bundles. Bake at 400 degrees for 30 minutes or until bacon is done and asparagus are tender.

Basil Garlic Mashed Potatoes

1. 5 Pounds of Red Potatoes (peeled and cut into small pieces)
2. 1 Container (8 oz.) Rondele Garlic and Herb Gourmet Spreadable Cheese
3. 3/4 Cup Milk (heated)
4. 3 Tablespoons Fresh Basil (chopped)

Cover potatoes with water and bring to a boil. Boil potatoes approximately 15 minutes or until tender. Drain and mash with electric mixer. Add spreadable cheese and milk and continue mixing. Fold in fresh basil. Keep warm until ready to serve.

Buttered Herbed Pasta

1. 1 Package (16 oz.) Wide Egg Noodles
2. 3 Tablespoons Butter
3. 1 Tablespoon Fresh Italian Parsley (chopped)
4. 2 Tablespoons Fresh Chives (chopped)

On stovetop, cook pasta according to package directions, al dente (pasta should be tender, but still firm, not mushy). Drain, and while pasta is still hot, toss with butter, fresh Italian parsley and fresh chives. Serve warm.

Corn On The Cob With Sizzle Butter

1. 8 Ears Fresh Corn on Cob
2. 1 Stick Butter (melted)
3. 2 Fresh Jalapeno Peppers (washed and seeded)
4. 1 Grated Lime Peel

In blender, coarsely chop jalapenos; add butter and lime peel. Process until smooth and place into a small serving bowl. Boil corn in salted water for approximately 8 minutes. Drain and serve with jalapeno lime butter. **Suggestion**: The jalapeno lime butter can be made a day ahead, refrigerated and brought to room temperature before serving.

Creamy Mashed Potatoes

1. **5 Pounds Potatoes**
2. **1 Package (4 oz.) Cream Cheese (softened)**
3. **1 Cup Prepared Dill Dip With Real Sour Cream**
4. **1 Cup Milk (heated)**

Peel, quarter, and rinse potatoes. On stovetop cook potatoes in boiling water until fork tender, soft but not mushy. Drain and place into large mixing bowl. Season to taste and add cream cheese, dill dip and milk. With electric mixer, beat until a creamy consistency. Place into casserole dish and serve. **Serving Idea**: Potatoes can be made ahead and reheated in the oven, covered, at 350 degrees for 30 minutes.

Explosive Broccoli Crowns

1. **2 Pounds Fresh Broccoli Crowns (cut in bite-size pieces)**
2. **1 Cup Caesar Ranch Flavored Gour Mayo**
3. **1 Tablespoon Roasted Garlic and Bell Pepper Seasoning**
4. **1 Cup Sharp Cheddar Cheese (grated)**

Wash and remove all tough stems from broccoli and cut into bite–size pieces. Mix mayo and seasoning. Toss with broccoli. Sprinkle grated cheese on top and refrigerate until ready to serve.

Fresh Basil, Tomato and Green Beans

1. 2-3 Large Tomatoes (sliced into 8 slices)
2. 1 Jar (18.7 oz.) Extra Fine Cooked Green Beans
3. 1 Container (4 oz.) Feta Cheese
4. Fresh Basil (snipped)

Refrigerate tomatoes and green beans so that they are chilled. Place tomato slices on serving platter. Divide the jar of green beans into 8 bundles. Place a bundle on top of each tomato slice. Sprinkle with fresh-snipped basil leaves and feta cheese. Refrigerate until ready to serve.

Hazelnut Brussels Sprouts

1. 2 Pounds Fresh Brussels Sprouts
2. 1/4 Cup Maple Syrup
3. 1/4 Cup Butter (melted)
4. 1/4 Cup Hazelnuts (chopped)

Wash Brussels sprouts and remove outer layer. Cut larger sprouts in half. Bring 8 cups of water to a boil and add the Brussels sprouts. Return to a boil and cook approximately 10 minutes or until sprouts are tender, but not mushy. Drain sprouts and place into an 8x8-inch casserole dish. In mixing bowl, combine maple syrup, butter and hazelnuts. Pour over sprouts and toss gently until coated. Serve warm.

Orange Cranberry Relish

1. 1 Bag (12 oz) Fresh Cranberries
2. 1 Jar (12 oz.) Orange Marmalade
3. 1/2 Cup Pecan Pieces
4. 1 Cup Sugar (dissolved in 1 cup water)

On stovetop simmer cranberries in 1-cup sugar and 1-cup water until the cranberries pop. Once they have popped remove from heat and mix in the orange marmalade and pecan pieces. Place into serving bowl and chill overnight or until ready to serve.

Parmesan Cauliflower

1. 2 Heads of Cauliflower
2. 1 Cup of Freshly Grated Parmesan Cheese
3. 1/3 Cup Mayonnaise
4. 2 Teaspoons Vegetable Supreme Seasoning (plus additional for top)

Wash cauliflower, remove stalks and cut into flowerets. Steam cauliflower until crisp tender. Combine mayonnaise, Parmesan cheese and 2 teaspoons vegetable seasoning. Place cooked cauliflower in large bowl and toss with mayonnaise/cheese mixture until all pieces are well coated. Place into microwave proof 1 1/2 quart casserole. Sprinkle top with vegetable seasoning. Cover and set aside. Immediately before serving, heat in microwave for 3 minutes or until warmed through.

Parsley New Potatoes and Pearl Onions

1. **2 Pounds Red New Potatoes**
2. **1 Pound White Pearl Onions**
3. **3 Tablespoons Extra Virgin Olive Oil**
4. **2 Tablespoons Fresh Rosemary (chopped)**

Preheat oven to 400 degrees. Wash and peel around center only of the new potatoes. Place into a lightly sprayed large casserole dish. Cut tips off pearl onions and peel away the outer skin of the onions and place into casserole with the potatoes. In small mixing bowl, combine olive oil and rosemary. Pour over potatoes and onions and mix until they are coated. Cover casserole and place into oven and bake at 400 degrees for 20 minutes. Turn potatoes and onions and continue baking an additional 20 minutes. Season to taste.

Peppered Pinto Beans

1. **1 Can (3 lb. 5 oz) Pinto Beans**
2. **2 Slices Peppered Bacon (cut into 1/2-inch strips)**
3. **1 1/2 Cups Beer**
4. **1/2 Cup Mild Picante Sauce**

In large skillet, sauté peppered bacon. Add beer and picante sauce. Reduce heat and simmer 2-3 minutes to reduce some of the fluid. Add beans and continue to simmer for 10 minutes or until beans are thoroughly heated.

Potato Bacon Casserole

1. 1 Package (28 oz.) Frozen Potatoes O'Brien
2. 6 Slices Peppered Bacon
3. 2 Cups Cheddar Cheese (grated)
4. 1 Cup Sour Cream

Preheat oven to 350 degrees. In a large skillet, fry bacon over medium heat, turning once. When bacon is crisp, remove from skillet and drain on a paper towel. Crumble bacon and set aside. Retain about 3 tablespoons of bacon grease in skillet and add frozen potatoes to the skillet. Turn heat to low and allow potatoes to cook for 10-12 minutes. Potatoes should be soft, but not browned, stir occasionally. Remove from heat and place into a large bowl. Add cheddar cheese, bacon, and sour cream. Mix well and place into a lightly sprayed casserole dish. Bake at 350 degrees for 1 hour.

Saucy Asparagus

1. 2 Pounds Asparagus (washed and tough larger ends removed)
2. 1 Package (1.25 oz.) Hollandaise Sauce Mix (prepared according to package directions. We used the one that requires water.)
3. 1/4 Cup Diced Roasted Red Peppers
4. 2 Teaspoons Fresh Lemon Juice

Add 3 tablespoons of water to a 9x13-inch microwave dish. Place asparagus in dish, thick stems facing center of dish, and cover with plastic wrap. Poke holes in wrap to vent. Microwave for 5 minutes or until crisp-tender. Drain. Prepare Hollandaise Sauce according to package directions. Add roasted red pepper and lemon juice to hollandaise sauce mix. Pour over asparagus and serve.

Savory Mushroom Dressing

1. **2 Jars (6 oz. each) Sliced Mushrooms (retain fluid – about 1/2 cup each jar)**
2. **2 Cans (14.5 oz. each) Chicken Broth**
3. **1 Stick Butter**
4. **1 Package (16 oz.) Pepperidge Farm Herbed Dressing**

On stovetop in large pan, heat mushrooms, mushroom fluid, chicken broth and butter until butter is melted. Add dressing mix and toss until all the dressing is moist and heated through. Place into a 1 1/2 quart baking dish. Serve immediately.

Sherried Wild Rice

1. **2 Boxes (6 oz. each) Original Uncle Ben's Wild Rice**
2. **1 Cup Celery (chopped)**
3. **1 Cup White Onion (chopped)**
4. **3/4 Cup Dry Cooking Sherry**

Cook rice according to package directions, but reduce water to 4 cups. Set aside. In large frying pan sprayed with cooking spray, add 1/4 cup cooking sherry. Add onions and celery and cook until softened. Add cooked rice and remainder of sherry. Mix together well, heat and serve. **Suggestion**: Can be made a day ahead and reheated before serving.

Southern Style Green Beans

1. 3 Cans (14 1/2 oz. each) Whole Green Beans
2. 8 Slices Center Cut Bacon (cooked and crumbled)
3. 1 Large Onion (chopped)
4. 1/3 Cup White Vinegar

On stovetop in large skillet, cook bacon until brown and crisp. Remove, drain and crumble bacon. Pour off all but 2 tablespoons drippings (leave in pan). Add onion to skillet along with vinegar and simmer for approximately 1 minute. Add drained green beans and mix with vinegar mixture. Season to taste. Add crumbled bacon and cook over low heat until heated. Serve warm.

Spicy Oven Fries

1. 2 Pounds Baking Potatoes
2. 2 Tablespoons Olive Oil
3. 2 Tablespoons Creole Seasoning
4. Parmesan Cheese (optional)

Cut each potato lengthwise into 8 wedges. Combine olive oil and Creole seasoning in a zip-top plastic bag. Add potato wedges and seal bag. Shake to coat potatoes. Arrange potato wedges, skin side down, in a single layer on a baking sheet coated with nonfat cooking spray. Bake at 450 degrees for 20 minutes or until golden brown. Remove from oven and sprinkle with Parmesan cheese if desired.

Spinach Casserole

1. 1 Package (8 oz.) Cream Cheese (softened)
2. 1 Package (16 oz.) Frozen Chopped Spinach (thawed and well drained)
3. 1 Can (8 oz.) Sliced Water Chestnuts (drained and chopped)
4. 1 Package (1.4 oz.) Knorr Vegetable Recipe Mix

Preheat oven to 350 degrees. Mix cream cheese, vegetable mix, and water chestnuts with drained spinach. Place into a lightly sprayed baking dish and bake at 350 degrees for 25 minutes.

Sweet Potato Casserole

1. 2 Cans (29 oz. each) Sweet Potatoes (drained, reserve 1/4 cup liquid)
2. 2 Tablespoons Pumpkin Pie Spice Mix
3. 1 Cup Pecan Pieces
4. 1 Bag (10 oz.) Toasted Coconut Marshmallows

Preheat oven to 350 degrees. In large bowl with electric mixer, mix potatoes and pumpkin spice mix together. Place into a lightly sprayed 9x13-inch casserole. Sprinkle pecan pieces on top of potatoes. Cut each toasted coconut marshmallow in half and press onto top of the sweet potato and pecans. Use entire bag, marshmallows should be touching each other. Bake at 350 degrees for 20 minutes or until heated through. Watch closely to make certain marshmallows don't burn.

Twice Baked Beans

1. **2 Cans (28 oz. each) Baked Beans with Bacon and Brown Sugar**
2. **6 Slices of Peppered Bacon (cut into 1-inch pieces)**
3. **1 Teaspoon Dry Mustard**
4. **1/2 Cup Ketchup**

Preheat oven to 350 degrees. Fry bacon until crisp, drain and break into pieces. Place beans, ketchup and mustard in crock-pot or baking dish. Stir to combine. Add bacon and toss to distribute. In oven, bake at 350 degrees for 30-45 minutes or until heated through. In crock-pot, cook on low for 3-4 hours.

Twice Baked Potatoes

1. **4 Large Baking Potatoes**
2. **1/2 Cup Sour Cream**
3. **1/2 Cup Milk (warmed)**
4. **4 Tablespoons Butter (melted)**

Preheat oven to 400 degrees. Wash and dry potatoes and lightly grease with vegetable oil or any oil you have in the cupboard. Bake for 1 hour or until tender. Remove from oven and set aside to cool slightly. Half potatoes lengthwise and carefully scoop flesh into a mixing bowl. Reserve skins for filling. Heat oven to 350 degrees. Whip milk, butter, sour cream and season to taste with potato flesh until mixture is smooth. Fill potato skins with mixture and bake at 350 degrees for 20-25 minutes or until heated through. **Suggestion**: Prepare potatoes ahead and refrigerate until ready to be heated prior to serving.

Yellow Squash Casserole

1. **6 Medium Yellow Squash (peeled and sliced)**
2. **1 Cup Chopped Onion**
3. **1 Cup Velveeta Cheese (cut into 1/2 inch cubes)**
4. **1 Can (4 oz.) Chopped Green Chiles**

Preheat oven to 375 degrees. Boil squash and onion until tender. Drain well and mix with cheese and chiles. Pour into buttered baking dish. Bake at 375 degrees for 15 minutes or until bubbly.

Zesty Carrots

1. **3 Pounds Raw Carrots (peeled and sliced 1-inch diagonally)**
2. **1 Bottle (11 oz.) GourMayo Wasabi Horseradish**
3. **1/2 Medium Onion (grated)**
4. **1 Bag (6 oz.) Buttery Garlic Croutons**

Preheat oven to 375 degrees. Cook carrots in seasoned boiling water, until crisp tender, approximately 10 minutes. Drain, reserving 1/2 cup liquid. Place carrots in an 8x8-inch baking dish. Combine reserved liquid, grated onion and mayonnaise and spread over carrots. Top with croutons. Bake at 375 degrees for 15 minutes. Do not over bake.

Baby Back BBQ Pork Ribs

1. **4-5 Pounds Baby Back Ribs (2 racks)**
2. **1 Can Beer**
3. **1/2 Cup Thai Peanut Sauce**
4. **1 Cup BBQ Sauce**

Preheat oven to 300 degrees. Form circle with each rack of ribs so that they stand up. Place ribs on rack and broiler pan, so that any fat can drip away. Place on lower rack in oven and bake for approximately 4 hours. While ribs are cooking, mix together beer, peanut sauce and BBQ sauce. Divide sauce into two separate bowls, one for basting ribs and the other to heat and serve as extra sauce with the ribs. Baste ribs every 30-45 minutes. Cover ribs for the last hour so that ribs do not dry out. Meat should fall away from bones. Serve with extra sauce.

Beef Roast With Vegetables

1. **5 Pounds Boneless Beef Shoulder Roast**
2. **2 Pounds Baby Carrots**
3. **2 Large White Onions (peeled and sliced)**
4. **1 Package (1 oz.) Dry Au Jus Mix**

Preheat oven to 350 degrees. Mix dry Au Jus Mix with 2 cups water. In frying pan sprayed with cooking spray, brown roast on both sides. Take out of frying pan and place roast into a roasting pan. Place carrots and onions around roast. Pour Au Jus Mix over roast. Cover and bake for 3 1/2 hours at 350 degrees. **Suggestion**: Left over Au Jus can be used for gravy over the potatoes.

Beef Tenderloin With Sherried Mushrooms

1. **4-5 Pounds Whole Beef Tenderloin**
2. **1 Pound Fresh Mushrooms (cleaned and sliced)**
3. **1 Cup Cooking Sherry**
4. **1 Tablespoon Minced Garlic**

Preheat oven to 425 degrees. Trim and remove fat and silver membrane from outside of tenderloin. Cut loin in half so it will fit in a large skillet. Generously spray bottom of large skillet with cooking spray and pre-heat to medium high. Place both pieces of tenderloin in preheated skillet and sear meat (approximately 2-3 minutes per side) or until brown. Remove meat from skillet and place onto a foil lined baking pan. Pour any remaining liquid from skillet over meat. Place into oven onto middle rack and bake at 425 degrees for 10 minutes per pound or until internal temperature of meat thermometer reaches 135 degrees for medium rare. The thinner piece of meat will be for those who like their meat cooked more. Remove from oven, cover with foil, and let stand 10 minutes before carving.

While tenderloin is cooking, sauté garlic (approximately 1 minute) in large skillet sprayed with cooking spray. Reduce heat and add mushrooms and continue to cook, stirring frequently, for approximately 4 minutes. Add sherry to mushrooms and simmer for 5 minutes reducing some of the liquid. Turn skillet off and let sherried mushrooms sit until ready to reheat. Prior to serving, quickly reheat mushrooms and serve with the tenderloin.

Buffalo Pork Loin

1. **1 (4-5 Pounds) Pork Loin Roast**
2. **1 Cup Prepared Buffalo Wing Sauce**
3. **1 Tablespoon Garlic Powder**
4. **1 Teaspoon Celery Salt**

Place pork loin in gallon size zip lock bag with the wing sauce. Marinate overnight. Preheat oven to 400 degrees. Remove roast with sauce and place on foil in shallow oven pan. Mix garlic powder and celery salt and sprinkle over top of roast. Bake uncovered at 400 degrees for 30 minutes. Reduce heat to 325 degrees and bake for 1 to 1 1/2 hours or until loin reaches an internal temperature of 170 degrees. Baste several times while loin is baking. Remove from oven and allow loin to rest for 20 minutes, before slicing and serving.

Dijon Glazed Corned Beef Sandwiches

1. **2 Containers (13.8 oz. each) Refrigerated Pizza Crust**
2. **1 1/2 Pounds Deli Sliced Corned Beef (3/4 lb. on each dough)**
3. **2 Packages (8 oz. each) Sliced Baby Swiss Cheese (1 package on each dough)**
4. **1/2 Cup Dijon Mustard (1/4 cup on each dough)**

Preheat oven to 400 degrees. Use two lightly sprayed 9x13-inch baking sheets. Place one crust on each baking sheet. Pat and spread dough until it is approximately the same size as the pan. Top each pizza crust with a layer of corned beef down the center of the dough. Top corned beef with a layer of cheese. Spread the mustard over the top of the cheese. Repeat layers ending with the mustard. Fold dough over the top of the meat and cheese and pinch dough together to seal. If necessary, moisten the dough with water to help seal. Repeat this process on the second pizza dough. Bake the sandwiches at 400 degrees for 20-25 minutes or until dough is golden brown. Remove and place sandwich rolls on wire rack to prevent bottom from being mushy. When slightly cooled and ready to serve, use a pizza cutter to slice into sandwiches.

Firecracker Chicken

1. **8 Boneless Skinless Chicken Breast Halves**
2. **2 Large Eggs plus 2 Tablespoons Water**
3. **1 Bag (13.25 oz.) Chile Limon Potato Chips (finely crushed)**
4. **1 Package (8 oz.) Monterrey Pepper Jack Cheese (cut into 8 slices, lengthwise)**

Preheat oven to 350 degrees. Remove as much visible fat from chicken as possible. Whisk eggs and water together until well combined. Dip chicken breast in egg mixture and then into crushed potato chips. Place on foil that has been lightly sprayed with cooking spray. Bake at 350 degrees for 40 minutes. Remove from oven and place cheese slices on top of each chicken breast. Return to oven for about 5 minutes or until cheese is melted.

Garlic Peppered Standing Rib Roast

1. **7 Pounds Standing Rib Roast Bone-In**
2. **2 Tablespoons Course Black Pepper**
3. **1 Teaspoon Lowry's Seasoned Salt**
4. **1 Teaspoon Garlic Powder**

Preheat oven to 450 degrees. Mix pepper, salt and garlic powder and rub on the standing rib roast. Place roast on a rack in a roasting pan. Bake uncovered at 450 degrees for 10 minutes. Reduce heat to 300 degrees and continue to bake uncovered for 2 to 2 1/2 hours. For a medium cooked roast, meat thermometer should reach 135 degrees when placed into center of roast. Remove roast from oven and cover with foil for 15 minutes before slicing.

Glazed Orange Ham

1. **1 Fully Cooked Spiral Cut Ham (6-8 Pounds)**
2. **1/3 Cup Mustard**
3. **1/2 Cup Firmly Packed Brown Sugar**
4. **1 Jar (18 oz.) Orange Marmalade**

Preheat oven to 350 degrees. Wrap the ham completely in foil and heat cut side down in shallow pan for 1 hour at 350 degrees. While ham is heating, combine the mustard, brown sugar and orange marmalade. Remove the ham from oven and remove foil. Increase oven temperature to 425 degrees and place ham, fat side up, back into pan. Brush and spoon orange marmalade sauce all over the ham. Return to oven and bake at 425 degrees for 10 minutes. Remove from oven and serve.

Laborless Oven Smoked Brisket

1. **5-6 Pounds Beef Brisket (well trimmed)**
2. **1/4 Cup Liquid Smoke**
3. **1 Teaspoon Fajita Seasoning**
4. **1/2 Cup Water**

Preheat oven to 275 degrees. Combine liquid smoke, fajita seasoning and water. Place brisket on large sheet of heavy-duty foil in a shallow roasting pan. Pour sauce over brisket and turn until well coated. Seal foil tightly. Bake at 275 degrees for 5 to 7 hours, about 1-1/4 hour per pound. Remove from oven and allow to rest for 15 minutes before slicing. **Helpful Hint**: It is important to let the brisket sit a little while before carving. This allows the juices to retreat back into the meat.

Roasted Herbed Turkey With Gravy

1. **1 (14-15 Pounds) Turkey (thawed according to package directions)**
2. **1 Stick Butter**
3. **2 Tablespoons Salt Free McCormick All-Purpose Seasoning (blend of herbs & spices)**
4. **6-8 Fresh Rosemary Springs (cut into 2-inch sprigs)**

Preheat oven to 325 degrees. Remove turkey from packaging. Remove giblet packaging from both inside turkey cavity and neck cavity. Rinse turkey and pat dry. Place turkey in roasting pan. In small saucepan, melt butter and mix in seasoning. Baste turkey with 1/2 of the melted herb butter. Place rosemary sprigs on top of the turkey breasts and legs. Place into oven and cook for 3 1/2 hours, uncovered, or until turkey is done. After turkey has cooked for 1 1/2 hours, baste it again with the remaining herb butter and cover top of turkey with aluminum foil to prevent top from browning too much. Remove from oven and let turkey sit for 15 minutes before carving. **Suggestion**: We recommend using a meat thermometer to take the guess out of knowing when the turkey is done.

Turkey Gravy: Place the turkey neck and giblets that you removed from the turkey cavities into a medium saucepan with 4 cups of salted water. Simmer over low heat for 1 1/2 to 2 hours to reduce the liquid down to about 2 cups. Remove neck and giblets; strain broth and return broth to saucepan. After removing turkey from oven, pour turkey drippings that are on the bottom of the roasting pan through a strainer and add 1 cup of these strained drippings to the broth. Whisk together 1/3 cup flour into 1 cup COLD water and stir until there are no lumps. Bring broth and drippings to a simmer and add the flour and water mixture. Continue cooking and stirring until mixture returns to a simmer. Simmer for 3-5 minutes. Add pepper to taste.

Rosemary Roasted Pork Tenderloin

1. **4 to 5 Pounds Boneless Pork Loin Roast**
2. **1/2 Cup Coarse Grained Mustard (we used Grey Poupon Country Dijon)**
3. **3 Tablespoons Balsamic Vinegar**
4. **2 Tablespoons Fresh Rosemary (chopped)**

Preheat oven to 375 degrees. Spray roasting pan with cooking spray and place roast into pan. Combine mustard, balsamic vinegar and rosemary. Spread over roast and bake at 375 degrees for 1 1/2 hours. Internal temperature needs to reach 160 degrees. Let stand for 10 minutes before serving. Place onto serving platter and garnish with fresh rosemary sprigs.

Salmon With Lemon Sauce

1. **2 Packages (16 oz. each) Frozen Salmon Fillets (thawed)**
2. **4 Tablespoons Mayonnaise**
3. **4 Tablespoons Fresh Lemon Juice**
4. **2 Teaspoon Dijon Mustard**

Preheat over to 375 degrees. Place salmon steaks onto a large lightly sprayed baking pan. Spray salmon steaks with cooking spray. Bake at 375 degrees for 8-12 minutes or until fish flakes when pierced with a fork. In a small bowl, mix the mayonnaise, fresh lemon juice and mustard to make the sauce. Refrigerate sauce until ready to serve with salmon.

Tamale Casserole

1. **3 Pounds Tamales (shucks removed and cut in 2-inch pieces)**
2. **1 Can (10 3/4 oz.) Cream of Chicken Soup**
3. **2 Cans (10 oz. each) Original Rotel Tomatoes and Green Chilies**
4. **2 Cups Monterrey Jack Cheese (grated)**

Preheat oven to 350 degrees. Place cut tamales in lightly greased casserole. Mix soup, Rotel tomatoes and 1 cup of cheese. Pour over tamales and sprinkle remaining cup of cheese over top of casserole. Bake at 350 degrees for 30 minutes or until bubbly.

Bleu Cheese Rolls

1. **1/4 Cup Butter**
2. **1/2 Cup Bleu Cheese Crumbles**
3. **2 Ounces Cream Cheese**
4. **2 Packages (11.3 oz each) Refrigerator Dinner Rolls**

Preheat oven to 400 degrees. In a saucepan, over low heat, melt butter, bleu cheese and cream cheese. Whisk together to combine. Cut rolls in half and dip each half into butter/cheese mixture. Place two roll halves into each cup of a standard muffin tin that has been sprayed with cooking spray. Bake at 400 degrees for 10-12 minutes.

Cinnamon Butter Rolls

1. **18 Rhodes Frozen Rolls**
2. **1/2 Stick Butter (melted)**
3 **2 Tablespoons Cinnamon/Sugar**
4. **1/4 Teaspoon Nutmeg**

Thaw rolls according to package directions. When thawed and risen, place on baking sheet. Preheat oven to 350 degrees. In saucepan, melt butter. Combine cinnamon/sugar, nutmeg and melted butter. Brush tops of rolls and bake at 350 degrees for 15-20 minutes. Remove rolls from baking sheet while they are still hot so they won't stick to the pan.

Harvest Bread Sticks

1. **2 Boxes (10.6 oz. each) Refrigerator Bread Sticks**
2. **3 Tablespoons Butter (melted)**
3. **Sesame Seeds**
4. **Pumpkin Seeds**

Preheat oven to 375 degrees. Remove breadsticks according to container directions. Roll each bread stick in melted butter and place on cookie sheet. Sprinkle with sesame seeds and pumpkin seeds. Bake at 375 degrees for 10-14 minutes.

Love Bread

1. 2 Cans (11 oz. each) Refrigerated Crusty French Loaf
2. 1/2 Stick Butter (melted)
3. 1 Tablespoon Dried Dill
4. 1/4 Cup Grated Parmesan Cheese

Preheat oven to 350 degrees. Open bread dough and place on cookie sheet. Form loaves to make a large heart shaped ring. Slice ends of the bread roll at a diagonal where they join to make the heart shape more accurately. Make sure the seam side of the bread roll is down. Pinch ends of bread together where they join. With a serrated knife, slice bread 2/3 of the way through loaf, every 1 to 1 1/2 inches. Melt butter and add dill. Brush loaf with butter mixture. Sprinkle cheese evenly around the top of the bread loaves. Bake at 350 degrees for 25-30 minutes, or until bread is golden brown. Serve on a flat platter to show off the heart design.

New Year's Eve Rolls

1. 2 Cans (11 oz.) Refrigerated Pillsbury French Loaf
2. 1/2 Cup Butter (melted)
3. 1 Tablespoon Italian Seasoning
4. 1 1/2 Teaspoons Garlic Powder

Preheat oven to 350 degrees. Remove bread dough from cans and slice each bread dough roll into 6 equal rounds. Place each slice on shallow baking dish or jellyroll pan. Combine melted butter, Italian seasoning and garlic powder. Brush each slice with butter mixture. Bake at 350 degrees for 20-25 minutes or until golden in color.

Rancher's Rolls

1. **18 Rhodes Frozen Rolls (thawed according to package directions)**
2. **1 Stick Unsalted Butter (melted)**
3. **1 Tablespoon Dry Ranch Dressing Mix**
4. **2 Tablespoons Fresh Parsley**

Preheat oven to 350 degrees. In small bowl, mix butter, ranch dressing mix and parsley. After rolls are thawed and before they have risen, cut each roll into 3 pieces and dip into butter mixture. Place into a lightly sprayed tube or bundt pan. When all rolls have been placed in pan, cover top with plastic wrap that has been sprayed with cooking spray. This will prevent tops of rolls from sticking to plastic wrap. Place in warm area of the kitchen and allow rolls to rise, approximately 3-4 hours or until doubled in size. Bake at 350 degrees for 15-20 minutes until golden brown.

Sunny Cheese Bread "Roses"

1. **2 Cans (8 oz. each) Refrigerated Crescent Rolls**
2. **2 Tablespoons Butter (melted)**
3. **1/2 Cup Sharp Cheddar Cheese (finely grated)**
4. **Sesame Seeds**

Preheat oven to 350 degrees. On waxed paper sprayed with cooking spray, unroll each crescent roll (don't separate into triangles). Each can makes 1 large rectangle. You should now have two large rectangles. Sprinkle each surface with 1/4 cup grated cheese. Starting at long side, roll each dough rectangle into long slender cylinder. Cut each cylinder into 12 equal slices. Place slices in lightly sprayed mini muffin tin, cut side up. Score top of each roll with a sharp knife in an "X." Brush with melted butter and sprinkle with sesame seeds. Bake at 350 degrees for 16-18 minutes.

Thanksgiving Rolls with Honey and Nut Butter

1. **2 Containers Refrigerated Rolls or Prepared Rolls**
2. **1/2 Cup Honey**
3. **1 Stick Butter (softened)**
4. **1/4 Cup Finely Chopped Pecans**

If using refrigerated rolls, bake according to container directions. Whip butter at medium speed with mixer until fluffy. Add honey and continue to beat until light and fluffy. Add nuts and mix thoroughly. Refrigerate until ready to serve with rolls.

Wreath of Rolls

1. **2 Cans (16.3 oz each) Jumbo Flaky Style Biscuits**
2. **1/2 Cup Butter (melted)**
3. **1 Tablespoon Finely Chopped Onion**
4. **2 Tablespoons Finely Chopped Fresh Chives**

Preheat oven to 350 degrees. In a bowl, combine the butter and onion. Open the can of biscuits and cut each biscuit in half. Brush each biscuit half in the butter mixture. On a lightly sprayed pizza pan, stand biscuits on their cut edge. With biscuits touching, arrange in a wreath type circle. Sprinkle with chives and bake at 350 degrees for 18-20 minutes or until biscuits are golden brown in color.

Angel Coconut Butter Cake

1. **1 Box (18.25 oz.) Butter Recipe Golden Cake Mix**
2. **2 Cups Sweetened Angel Flake Coconut**
3. **2 Cups Sour Cream**
4. **1 Container (8 oz.) Cool Whip**

Bake cake mix according to package directions using two cake pans. Allow to cool completely. When cool, split layers to make four layers. In bowl, mix the coconut and sour cream. Set aside 1 cup of this mixture to use in the frosting. Use the remainder to frost in between layers of cake. Fold the 1 cup of reserved coconut mixture into the Cool Whip. Frost top and sides of the cake. Cover and refrigerate until ready to serve. **Helpful Hint**: Dental floss is a great tool for cutting through a layered cake. Simply take a long piece of dental floss, pull it taut and saw through.

Apple Carrot Cake

1. 1 (18.25 oz.) Super Moist Carrot Cake Mix
2. 1 Cup Fresh Apples (peeled and chopped)
3. 1/2 Cup Chopped Pecans
4. 1 Can (16 oz.) Cream Cheese Frosting

Preheat oven to 350 degrees. Mix and prepare carrot cake mix according to package directions. Add apples and pecans to mixture. Pour mixture into two lightly sprayed 8-inch cake pans and bake at 350 degrees for 27-32 minutes. Allow to cool for 5 minutes before removing from pan. Allow to cool completely before frosting with cream cheese frosting. **Serving Idea**: Decorate frosted cake with pecans.

Butter Pecan Pie - Chocolate Crumb Pie Shell

1. 1/2 Gallon Butter Pecan Ice Cream
2. 3 Tablespoons Hershey's Classic Caramel Topping
3. 3 Tablespoons Heath Shell Chocolate with Toffee Bits
4. 1 Can Whipped Heavy Cream (Land O Lakes)

Soften ice cream at room temperature. Place one-half of the softened ice cream into chocolate crumb pie shell. Drizzle caramel topping over ice cream. Place other half of the ice cream on top of caramel. Drizzle chocolate over ice cream and cover. Put back in freezer until ready to serve. Five minutes before you are ready to serve pie, remove from freezer. Slice into serving pieces and top each piece with whipped cream.

Championship Brownies

1. 1 Box (19.8 oz.) Brownie Mix (baked according to package directions)
2. 36 Caramels (unwrapped)
3. 1/2 Cup Whipping Cream
4. 1 Cup Pecan Pieces

Bake brownies according to package directions, remove from oven and allow the brownies to cool for 15 minutes. While brownies are baking, combine caramels and cream in medium saucepan and cook over low heat until caramels are melted and the mixture is smooth, stirring occasionally. Add pecans and stir until the nuts are well coated. Remove from heat. Spread caramel pecan layer over baked brownies. Cool to room temperature. Cover and refrigerate until caramel is set, approximately 45 minutes.

Double Chocolate Trifle

1. 1 Box (19.8 oz.) Fudge Brownie Mix
2. 2 Containers (22 oz. each) Prepared Chocolate Pudding
3. 1 Container (12 oz.) Extra Creamy Cool Whip
4. 1 Package (8 oz.) Heath English Toffee Bits

Bake brownie mix according to package directions for cake-like brownies. Allow to completely cool. Divide brownies into thirds. Remove from pan and tear into bite-size pieces. Place a layer of brownies on the bottom of a trifle bowl, followed by a layer of pudding, cool whip and candy bits. Repeat layers twice, ending with candy. Cover with plastic wrap and refrigerate until ready to serve.

Cherries Jubilee With Ice Cream

1. **2 Cans (16 oz. each) Pitted Dark Sweet Cherries**
2. **1/2 Cup Sugar**
3. **1/4 Cup Cornstarch**
4. **1/2 Cup Brandy**

Drain cherries, reserving syrup. On stovetop in saucepan, blend sugar and cornstarch. Gradually stir in reserved syrup, mixing well. Cook and stir over medium heat until mixture is thickened and bubbly. Remove from heat, stir in cherries. Turn mixture into a chafing dish or blazer pan. Place chafing dish at the dinner table along with individual bowls of ice cream for your guests. Heat brandy in small saucepan. Pour heated brandy into a large ladle. At the table, ignite the brandy so it flames. While it is flaming, pour onto the cherries jubilee. Stir to blend brandy into the sauce. **Note**: Brandy will continue to flame for a while, even while you serve the cherries jubilee over the ice cream.

Chocolate Chunk Peanut Butter Cookies

1. **1 Jar (18 oz.) Peanut Butter**
2. **1 1/4 Cups Sugar**
3. **2 Eggs (room temperature)**
4. **1 Bag (10 oz.) Dark Chocolate Chunks (Nestle)**

Preheat oven to 350 degrees. Combine peanut butter, sugar and eggs in a mixing bowl. Beat with mixer until sugar becomes smooth, about 3 minutes. Chop chocolate chunks into smaller chunks and combine with the peanut butter mixture. Form into about 1-inch balls and place onto an ungreased cookie sheet. Press down on the center of each ball and bake at 350 degrees for 10-12 minutes or until lightly browned. Remove from oven and cool on a wire rack.

Chocolate Fondue

1. **1 Package (12 oz.) Semisweet Chocolate Morsels**
2. **3/4 Cup Whipping Cream**
3. **1 Bag (8 oz.) Peanut Brittle**
4. **1 Bag (10 oz.) Pretzel Rods**

In a medium microwave safe bowl, combine chocolate morsels and whipping cream. Microwave on high for 1 minute, stirring once. Remove from microwave and whisk until smooth. Place into a fondue pot and serve with pieces of peanut brittle and pretzel rods. **Suggestion**: You can have your guests dip their own peanut brittle or pretzel rods, or you can dip a few and place on a plate near the fondue pot.

Eggnog Panettoni Bread Pudding With Sauce

1. **5 Cups Panettoni Bread (cut into very small pieces)**
2. **1/2 Cup Pecan Pieces or Walnut Pieces**
3. **3 Cups plus 1 Cup (for sauce) Prepared Eggnog**
4. **1/3 Cup plus 2 Teaspoons (for sauce) Bourbon**

Preheat oven to 475 degrees. On stovetop, heat a pot of water (approximately 2 cups) for use later. In a large mixing bowl, combine panettoni bread pieces, nut pieces, 3 cups eggnog and 1/3 cup bourbon. Spray a 12 hole muffin tin with cooking spray and ladle bread/eggnog mixture evenly into the muffin tins. Top surface will not be smooth. Place muffin tin onto a baking sheet with sides. Place into preheated oven and pour the heated water into the baking sheet around the muffin tin. This creates a water bath around the muffin tin. Bake at 475 degrees for 15-20 minutes until the tops are nicely browned and a toothpick comes clean from the center. Remove muffin tin from oven. Safety warning: Leave water in oven on the baking sheet to cool. Let the bread pudding cool slightly before removing from the tins. **Suggestion**: Bread pudding can be made earlier in the day.

Sauce for Bread Pudding: On stovetop combine the remaining 1 cup eggnog and 2 teaspoons bourbon in a saucepan and heat until warm, but not boiling. Serve hot on top of bread pudding.

Gingerbread Cookies

1. 1 Box (10.25 oz.) Moist Deluxe Spice Cake Mix
2. 1 Teaspoon Ginger
3. 2 Egg Yolks (room temperature)
4. 3/4 Cups Butter

Preheat oven to 375 degrees. In mixing bowl, cream the butter and add the egg yolks and continue to mix. Add the ginger and cake mix into butter and yolks, and mix until well combined. Dough is very stiff. Place dough on a lightly floured surface. Pat dough into a flat circle. Cover with a sheet of wax paper; and with a rolling pin, roll dough out into 1/8-inch thickness. With a round cookie cutter, cut cookies and place 2-inches apart on a lightly sprayed cookie sheet. Bake at 375 degrees for 10 minutes or until slightly browned. Remove to wire rack to cool.

Lemonade Pudding

1. 1 Can (6 oz.) Frozen Lemonade (thawed)
2. 1 Can (14 oz.) Sweetened Condensed Milk
3. 1 Carton (8 oz.) Cool Whip
4. 1 Package (14 oz.) Mother's Iced Lemonade Cookies

Crush cookies (about 24) into crumbs and divide crumbs into thirds. In a 8x8-inch baking dish, sprinkle 1/3 crumbs in bottom of dish. In mixing bowl, combine milk, cool whip and lemonade together. Spread 1/2 cup lemonade mixture on top of cookie crumbs. Sprinkle another layer of crumbs and then the remainder of lemonade mixture. Top with remaining third of crumbs. Refrigerate at least one hour or until firm.

Nutty Lemon Cookies

1. 1 Container (16.5 oz) Refrigerator Sugar Cookie Dough
2. 1 Cup Chopped Pecans
3. 1 Tablespoon Grated Lemon Peel
4. 3/4 Cup Powdered Sugar

Preheat oven to 375 degrees. Place cookie dough into a mixing bowl. Add pecans and lemon peel and stir until well blended. On a sprayed cookie sheet, drop cookie dough by tablespoon (walnut size) and bake at 375 degrees for 10-12 minutes or until very lightly browned. Cool 2 minutes on a cookie sheet and then remove to wire rack. Place powdered sugar in a bowl and dip warm cookies in the powdered sugar. Place back on wire rack and cool completely.

Orange Angel Food Cake

1. 1 Package (16 oz.) Angel Food Cake Mix
2. 2/3 Cup Frozen Orange Juice Concentrate (thawed)
3. 1 Container (12 oz.) Cool Whip
4. 1/4 Cup Plain Yogurt

Prepare Angel Food Cake as directed on package, but pour 1/3 cup of thawed orange juice into a 2-cup measure and add enough water for the mixture to equal the amount of water called for in the package directions. Bake according to directions. Cool completely. Combine Cool Whip, yogurt and remaining 1/3 cup orange juice concentrate. Frost top and sides of cake. Cover and refrigerate until ready to serve.

Pecan Pie

1. **3 Eggs (beaten)**
2. **1 Cup Sugar**
3. **3/4 Cup White Corn Syrup**
4. **1 Cup Chopped Pecans**

Preheat oven to 325 degrees. Mix all the above ingredients and place into unbaked pie shell. Bake at 325 degrees for 1 hour or until inserted knife comes out clean. **Helpful Hint**: Make pie in advance.

Praline Cookie Squares

1. **14-15 Cinnamon Graham Cracker Cookies**
2. **1 Cup Butter**
3. **1 Cup Light Brown Sugar**
4. **1 1/2 Cups Chopped Pecans**

Preheat oven to 350 degrees. Lightly spray a 15x10x1-inch jellyroll pan. Place enough graham crackers on pan to cover. In saucepan bring butter, brown sugar and pecans to a boil. Boil 2 minutes, stirring constantly. Remove from heat and spread over the tops of the graham crackers. Bake at 350 degrees for 10 minutes. Remove from oven and cool. When cooled, cut into squares.

Pumpkin Pie

Unbaked Pie Shell

1. 1 Can (16 oz.) Pumpkin
2. 1 Can (14 oz.) Sweetened Condensed Milk
3. 2 Eggs (beaten)
4. 1 Teaspoon Pumpkin Pie Spice

Preheat oven to 425 degrees. Combine all the above ingredients and mix well. Pour into unbaked pie shell. Bake 15 minutes at 425 degrees; then reduce heat to 350 degrees and bake an additional 35-40 minutes. **Helpful Hint**: Make pie in advance.

Sparkling Fireworks Dessert

1. 1 Bottle (1 oz.) Orange Extract
2. 8 Sugar Cubes
3. 1/2 Gallon Vanilla Ice Cream
4. Chocolate Syrup

Place ice cream balls into eight individual serving dishes. Top with chocolate syrup. Pour orange extract into a small condiment dish. Toss each sugar cube individually in the orange extract making sure cube is well saturated. Place one sugar cube on top of each ice cream ball. After all guests are served, using a long stem lighter, light each sugar cube. Orange soaked sugar cube will flame for a very effective New Year's finale. **Helpful Hint**: You may want to practice lighting an orange extract sugar cube, so you will know what to expect. **Helpful Hint**: The day before, freeze scoops of ice cream balls and place on wax paper in an airtight container. Place in the freezer. Margarita glasses make a festive serving dish.

Strawberries and Cream Dessert

1. **2 Quarts Fresh Strawberries (washed, dried and sliced)**
2. **1/4 Cup Sugar**
3. **1/2 Cup Cream de Cocoa**
4. **1 Can (14 oz.) Land O Lake Creamy Whipped Cream (sprayed from can)**

To make a thick cream, in a large mixing bowl, spray whipped cream from the container to fill the bowl. Add sugar and Cream de Cocoa and stir to the consistency of a thick cream (not as thick as cool whip). If needed more whipped cream can be added. Gently fold the strawberries into the cream. Serve in individual parfait glasses or small bowls.

Strawberry Dessert

1. **1 (18.25 oz.) Strawberry Cake Mix**
2. **1 Cup Cool Whip for Cake Mix and 3 Cups for Frosting**
3. **3 Egg Whites**
4. **1 Can (21 oz.) Strawberry Pie Filling**

Preheat oven to 350 degrees. Combine cake mix, 1 cup cool whip and 1 cup water. Pour 1/2 of the batter into greased 9 x 13-inch cake pan. Open can of strawberry pie filling and with a fork, remove the whole strawberries, leaving the remaining filling to be used for the topping. Distribute the strawberries over the cake batter and cover with the remaining batter. Bake at 350 degrees for 35-40 minutes or until cake is done. Allow to cool. **Helpful Hint**: An 8 oz. tub of Cool Whip yields 3 cups of Cool Whip. A 12 oz. tub yields 4 1/2 cups; and a 16 oz. tub yields 6 1/2 cups of Cool Whip.

For frosting: Add 1/4 cup of the pie filling to 3 cups of cool whip and combine. You can leave the cake in the pan and frost the top or remove from the pan and frost the top and sides. Place the remaining pie filling in a sandwich bag and cut off one small corner of the bag and "pipe" the glaze across the top of the frosting in any design that you prefer. Cover and refrigerate until ready to serve.

Index

A

Appetizers

Cakes

Chicken

Cookies

D

Desserts

E

F

G

H

O

P

Pie

Pork

R

S

Salads

Seafood

Shopping Lists

Sides – See Vegetables And Sides

<u>**Soups**</u>

<u>**T**</u>

<u>**V**</u>

<u>**Vegetables And Sides**</u>

The Four Ingredient Cookbooks

Please send me…

The Four Ingredient Cookbooks® Holidays & Celebrations ____ copies @ $19.95 each $_____

The Four Ingredient Cookbooks®   ____ copies @ $19.95 each $_____

The Diabetic Four Ingredient Cookbook®   ____ copies @ $19.95 each $_____

Postage & handling @ $3.50 each $_____

Sub-Total $_____

Texas residents add 8.25% sales tax per book @ $1.93 each $_____

Canadian orders add additional $6.60 per book $_____

Total Enclosed $_____

❑ Check enclosed made payable to "Coffee and Cale"

Or charge to my

❑ VISA   ❑ MasterCard   ❑ Discover   *(Canada - credit card only)*

Card #_____   Exp. Date _____

Ship to:

Name _____

Address_____Apt.# _____

City _____ State_____ Zip _____

E-mail address_____

Phone_____
          (Must have for Credit Card Orders)

NOTES

NOTES

NOTES

NOTES

NOTES